"WHO ATE THE BACKYARD?"

LIVING WITH

WILDLIFE

ON PRIVATE LANDS

by Charles S. Craighead

Illustrated by Lawrence Ormsby

photography by Tom Mangelsen, Sandy and Allan Carey, Franz Camenzind,
Shane Moore, W.E. Dilley and Greg Winston

published by
Grand Teton Natural History Association
and the Jackson Hole Wildlife Foundation
in cooperation with the National Park Service

ISBN 0-931895-48-0

Illustrations ©1997 Lawrence Ormsby, Wilson, Wyoming, 83014.

Text ©1997 Charles Craighead, Moose, WY 83012.

Design, maps and production: Carole Thickstun

Editing: Just Write

Production Coordination: Sharlene Milligan, Executive Director, Grand Teton Natural History Association

Photography:
Franz Camenzind: p. 21, 34 (top and middle), 44, 45 (bottom)
Alan and Sandy Carey: p. 32 (top), 34 (bottom), 43, 45 (top), 55, 78, 95, 97 (bottom)
W. E. Dilley: p. 28, 48 (top), 85
Tom Mangelsen: p. 8, 14, 15, 17, 18, 19, 22, 30, 41 (top and bottom), 81, 97 (top)
Patrick Matheny: p. 60
Shane Moore: p. 63
National Park Service: p. 23
Diana Stratton: p. 6
Kathy Watkins: p. 11
Greg Winston: p. 9, 12, 32 (bottom), 37, 39, 48 (middle), 62
University of Wyoming: p. 66

Financial support of this book comes in part by grants from the Scott Opler Foundation.

I would like to thank Tom and Meredith Campbell of the Jackson Hole Wildlife Foundation for inviting me into this project.
Thanks to the four Toms: Tom Campbell, Tom Bills, Tom Segerstrom and Tom Toman for reading the text and contributing their knowledge. A special thanks to Tom Bills, who graciously gave me all of his research material on this subject, supported my effort, and provided me with invaluable contacts and ideas.
I appreciate the efforts of everyone who contributed their interesting experiences with wild animals. I wish there was room for every story.
Sharlene Milligan and the Board of Directors of the Grand Teton Natural History Association who were extremely supportive and encouraging throughout the project.
Thanks to the photographers, who patiently waited while we decided which images to use, and to Carole and Lawrence for making it all look good.
And thanks to the early pioneers of Jackson Hole, who established a way of life that included the peaceful interaction with wildlife as an everyday occurrence.
   Charlie Craighead, Moose, Wyoming

I would like to thank the following people for their help in the book:
Susan Tasaki, for teaching me to dream the book I want to read, and then try to create it;
Lorna Miller, for encouragement, great generosity and living the co-existence with the wildlife ideal;
Don Albrecht, for his generosity to the wildlife that live on his land and artists that need a space to create;
And Waldo Smith, for opening my eyes to wildlife.
   Carole Thickstun,
   Ormsby & Thickstun Design

Table of Contents

Coyote Pups

Introduction

Nearly everyone has a story about an animal that got into the house or chewed up a garden or bored a hole in the wall. We've all heard rustlings in the night and found strange tracks or tooth marks, and we've smelled the full range of wild smells from skunks to dead mice. We've fed hungry birds in the winter and cursed gophers in the summer. Part of living in a rural or suburban home is learning about wildlife.

Unfortunately, the way we react to wildlife is often the result of our misconceptions about their behavior or biology. Instead of helping them we hurt them, though we may not know it. When we offer the wrong food, inadvertently lure them into yards, let our pets chase them, or fail to recognize what elements of their habitat we have taken, we do more harm than if we ignore them. Our goal with this book is to minimize, when we can, the impact of civilization on wildlife through encouragement and proper discouragement of wild species on private property. It is offered as a guide to responsible co-existence.

The information presented here will apply to many geographic areas, but the focus of this book centers on the mountainous region of northwestern Wyoming and includes Montana, Idaho, Utah and Colorado. These five states encompass a diverse area, a haven for wildlife, a place where houses and developments often conflict with wildlife habitat. Much of the West is tied up in public land administered by the U.S. Forest Service, National Park Service, and the Bureau of Land Management, so some of the neighboring private land benefits from the protection of these agencies by being inhabited by wildlife.

Living in an area with abundant wildlife brings certain obligations, mainly learning about the plants and animals just as you would learn a region's climate, politics, and social customs. Whether you want to encourage deer to winter near you, rid your home of unwelcome rodents, or build a fence that is wildlife-friendly, the first step is information.

We suggest defensive measures rather than offensive ones. Protect your garden instead of poisoning rodents that enter it; plant native vegetation that can withstand browsing by wildlife; seal your home to mice and squirrels and allow predators to keep rodents in check outdoors; plant trees to mark your property lines instead of erecting fences.

There are recommendations and suggestions contained in this book for living with wildlife, but there are always exceptions to the rules. One of the fascinating things about wild animals is that their behavior is so unpredictable; a plant one homeowner finds unpalatable to deer may be devoured by a herd of deer in another yard.

We hope you will think about the consequences to wildlife of your actions in building and maintaining a home. If there is an alternative that is less harmful, or even beneficial to wildlife, do it.

CHAPTER ONE

Moose

Moose are big, gangly members of the deer family with unmistakable features. They migrate seasonally from higher to lower elevations and move from one type of forage to another. They prefer to eat fresh shoots and aquatic vegetation in the summer and feed on willows, tree bark, and other woody plants,

including spruce and fir needles, in winter. Willows are their staple all year long. Moose are generally solitary, living alone or in family groups of two and three, but bulls do not remain with the cows. After the mating season in late fall the bulls tend to gather into small groups. The mating season occurs in September and October, when the bulls will guard successive individual cows while they mate. The calves, one or two per cow, will be born in May or June. In late winter and early spring moose will begin to shed great patches of winter hair and gain the typical "mangy moose" look.

Moose are particularly susceptible to wood ticks in winter and may be covered with hundreds of them. A tick-covered moose will leave bloody spots on the snow where it beds down and may be more irritable than usual.

If a winter is severe moose may find themselves grouping up where food is available. Moose seem to like a free meal and often show up where livestock is being fed, aggressively competing for food with the livestock and with each other.

MOOSE
RANGE

Alces alces

MOOSE ON THE PROPERTY: During the spring and summer, conflicts with moose usually involve cow moose with calves. The cows seek out dense thickets or timbered areas to give birth, and they will remain in this territory for several months. Cow moose are extremely aggressive and will not only defend their calves but will chase intruders on a whim, so walking with a dog in moose habitat often invites trouble for both you and the dog.

If you have a cow and calf moose on or near your property, the best thing to do is leave them alone. If there are moose in the general area and you are uncertain where there are calves, you should use extra caution when walking in areas of thicker vegetation, especially willow thickets or other wetland growth. If a cow and calf are using an area necessary for human use, like a driveway or a yard, they can be chased off with loud noises and visual means like a waving cloth. This should be done from a respectful distance and with a planned escape route to safety. Continued disturbance over a number of days

Bull Moose at Taggart Lake

will usually move the moose, but they tend to return.

One of the reasons moose appear in yards and driveways in winter is the ease of travel in those places. Despite their long legs and big feet moose can have a difficult time in the deep snow. Winter travel is stressful and exhausting for wildlife, and once a moose finds a nicely plowed drive or a sheltered yard full of landscaped plants it will be reluctant to leave.

Moose that are fed hay in a backyard become tolerant of people and seem tame, but they retain an unpredictable temperament. Notorious for their bad tempers and sometimes aggressive behavior, moose are generally unafraid and will kill dogs, kick horses and cattle and chase humans. Moose become possessive of their source of handouts and will "demand" to be fed, a habit that extends to neighboring properties as well.

FEEDING: Don't feed the moose. Like other wild animals they will become dependent on a food source even when it does not nourish them properly. Studies have shown that a moose's digestive system is adapted to rich natural forage, skimming the nutrients and passing the woody roughage, as opposed to a domestic cow, which relies on a long digestive process to get nutrients from a relatively poor food. That's why moose are constantly eating. In winter a moose's energy requirements increase greatly and they can be easily exhausted if chased through deep snow. Moose are better off fending for themselves. *(see Artificial Feeding p. 14)*

SIGNS OF MOOSE: If there are moose in the yard you can't miss them, but sometimes they feed in your yard at night and then move off to rest in more dense growth during the day. Typical moose signs include a well-trampled yard; thrashed and broken vegetation, especially shrubs like willows and aspens (moose and other deer don't have upper incisor teeth so they can't bite off vegetation cleanly, and must twist and pull twigs and leaves from trees); piles of moose droppings (inch-long, fat, oval-shaped pellets); and big, deerlike tracks about five or six inches long and four inches wide.

MOOSE AND LANDSCAPING: In winter moose live on woody plants like aspens, willows and other shrubs. They will also gnaw off tree bark and eat spruce or pine needles, but unless really hungry will pass up Russian olive, juniper, raspberry, or lilac. *(see Landscaping, p. 86)* If moose are regular visitors to your home you can either try to fence them out, plant more of whatever you find they don't like to eat, or plant native vegetation that recovers from being browsed. Moose are attracted to commercial fertilizers and salt used for melting ice on sidewalks, so avoid using these products.

MOOSE AND FENCES: Moose are tall enough to negotiate most fences, but their long hind legs are often caught in barbed wire as they step over. If moose move across your property, you should remove unnecessary fences and consider altering the others, especially wire fences. *(See Fences p. 32)* In deep snow moose and other animals tend to try to cross a fence wherever they meet it rather than move along it looking for an opening. Let-down panels will work only if they are on a well-used pathway.

ATTRACTING MOOSE: Obviously, moose should not be attracted to an area they would not normally inhabit. Moose are independent, solitary animals, but encouraging the growth of browse species like willows for winter use may keep animals in an area where it is safe to view them from a distance. The farther this planting is from dwellings the better. Moose have good memories for food, so once they find it they will continue to show up.

DISCOURAGING MOOSE: The absence of food will keep moose moving, and loud noise and other disturbances will usually discourage them. However, a hungry and belligerent moose can be almost impervious to gunfire, car horns, and barking dogs. One method that seems to work when others fail is to run a small engine, such as a chainsaw or snowmobile nearby. Moose that would not respond to other loud noises have been slowly moved along from a safe distance by a running engine. Moose should never be chased with a snowmobile, however. Care must be taken in driving animals off so that they are moved safely and slowly enough to prevent exhaustion. Avoid using salt on roads and walkways and use plant fertilizer in solution form only.

Foods of Importance to Moose *(Each moose consumes approx. 25 lbs. per day)*	TREE	SHRUB
Willow (*Salix* spp.)		
Aspen (*Populus tremuloides*)		
Spruce (*Picea* spp.)		
Fir (*Abies* spp.)		
Sagebrush (*Artemisia* spp.)		
Bitterbrush (*Purshia* spp.)		

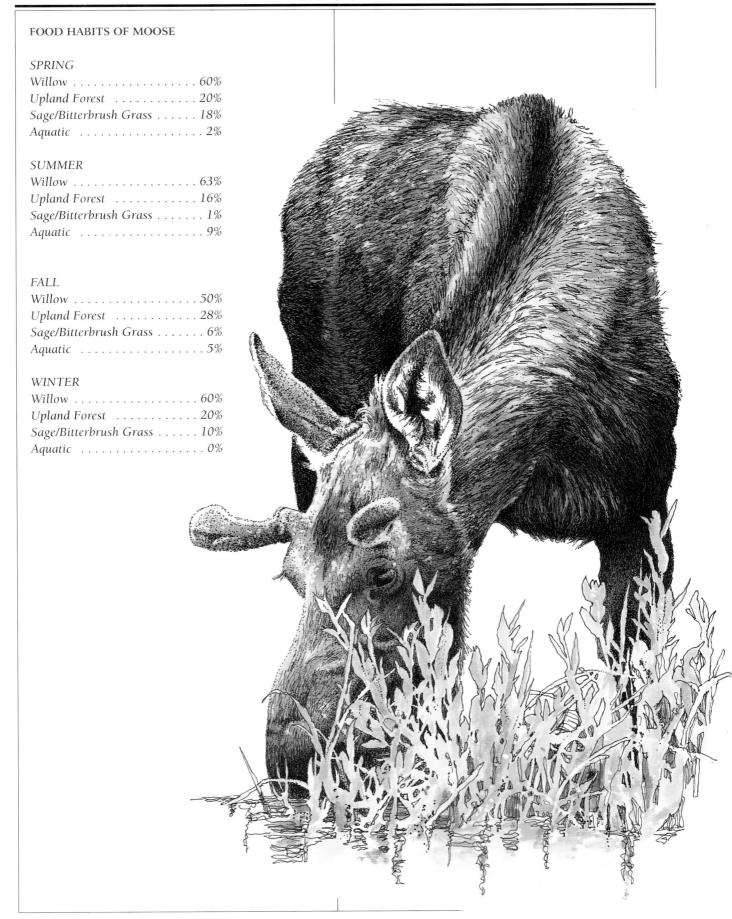

FOOD HABITS OF MOOSE

SPRING
Willow *60%*
Upland Forest *20%*
Sage/Bitterbrush Grass *18%*
Aquatic *2%*

SUMMER
Willow *63%*
Upland Forest *16%*
Sage/Bitterbrush Grass *1%*
Aquatic *9%*

FALL
Willow *50%*
Upland Forest *28%*
Sage/Bitterbrush Grass *6%*
Aquatic *5%*

WINTER
Willow *60%*
Upland Forest *20%*
Sage/Bitterbrush Grass *10%*
Aquatic *0%*

The Moose and the Swingset

We live in the Teton foothills, south of Wilson, Wyoming. Originally, I suppose, the moose had these hills to themselves. Then people came, building roads and houses. The moose have adapted to our human intrusions and still live with us, moseying from undisturbed hillsides to driveways and yards, munching on whatever seems palatable to a moose.

Last May a young cow wandered up our driveway early one morning. Following on her heels, a shaky-legged rusty brown calf stared wide-eyed at our human trappings. We watched these two with awe from the safety of our picture windows, and laughed with delight as the youngster took a big sniff of my red geraniums decorating the deck. Later, as they ambled around the garage and on to the neighbor's yard, we warned each other to keep an eye open for the new mother and her calf when we were hiking around the area. Nothing is more protective of its young than a 800-pound cow moose!

We didn't see the pair again until late August. My, how the calf had grown! He gamboled around the yard with much enthusiasm, occasionally running into the cow. As for mom, she looked just plain pooped. It seemed obvious to us that keeping this bundle of energy out of trouble was wearing her out and making her cranky. The calf persisted in trying to get the cow to join in his play; she reacted with a quick nip to his hind quarters as he passed by. Startled, the calf loped off—to be confronted by a fearsome enemy!

My daughter's large, metal swing set stood silently in the sun, and it captured his full attention. Laying back his ears and raising the fur on his neck, the calf stalked toward the swing set. Then, the attack! With front feet flying, the calf battered this scary foe: he charged, he snorted, he mouthed the

plastic-covered chains of the swings! He would prance off, panting from the fight, then charge in again to resume the fray.

We laughed and laughed, and bemoaned the fact that we did not own a video camera, for this would surely be winning footage for *Funniest Home Videos*.

During one pause in the action, my husband had a startling thought: what if little calf got his foot or leg caught in one of the swings, or the trapeze? It was certain that the cow—who had lain down in the shade for a nap with junior so busily occupied—would be quick to defend her calf from any human approach. So, we watched and fretted, and finally the calf, confident that he had won this battle, wandered off to nibble on a nearby shrub. My husband sneaked out the basement door, scuttled to the swing set, and rolled up the dangling swings just in case calf moose returned for round two.

A bit later, cow moose got up from her nap and began to wander out of the yard. Calf followed docilely behind, a proud lift to his head as the conqueror of this backyard.

Two more times in the fall before the snows came, the cow and calf paid us a visit, munching on the plants and shrubs that cover most of our two acres. The calf always checked the swing set, but there was no need for further attacks.

Humbled, the swing set offered no resistance to this little king of the hills.

By Linda Olson
Grand Teton
National Park
Moose, WY

The Moose That Went Trick or Treating

"Let's carve them!" said Mike.

"Let's paint them!" said Chris.

The two boys were deciding what to do with the pumpkins that their mom had just brought home. The house was almost decorated for Halloween. Witches, black cats, and spider webs were all over. But the most important thing, the pumpkins, had not been done.

Mike and Chris live in Grand Teton National Park. The Park is home to a great many animals, including bear, elk, deer and others. Most had already moved south, out of the park, with the coming winter. The only large animal around was moose.

With snow already on the ground, food was becoming harder and harder for the moose to find. One cow moose would take her twin calves and eat the grass from the lawn of Mike and Chris' house. The boys loved to see Molly and her twins, even if Mom complained about the fact that they ate the flowers in her garden and the leaves off the aspen tree.

"We'll paint pumpkins this year," Mom said. "Chris is only three and does not need to carve pumpkins with big knives." So the boys got out their paints and markers and decorated the pumpkins.

Mike made his pumpkin look very scary. It had missing teeth and a mean face.

Chris' pumpkin looked kind of friendly. Chris did not like scary things.

So Halloween came. Everyone was excited. Mike was having a big party at school. Chris was getting his costume ready and both were looking forward to Trick or Treating.

"Look, your first Trick or Treaters!" said their mom that morning. Standing by the door was Molly the Moose.

"Moose don't Trick or Treat, Mom," said Mike.

"I hope you are right," said Mom. "I don't want to see what kind of trick they would play."

After school everything was ready for the children who would be coming to the house for their treats. "Let's put our pumpkins outside so everyone can see them!" yelled Mike.

"Yeah!" answered Chris. So they took their pumpkins and put them out on the picnic table.

When the boys got back from trick or treating,
they were so excited they forgot to bring their pumpkins back inside. It really didn't matter. What could happen to them over night?

Halloween night was very cold in the mountains. Molly and her babies were hungry when they woke up. Where could they find something to eat? Molly remembered the house at the end of the street. There was still some grass not covered by snow there.

Off she went, followed by the two calves. When she got to the house, something odd was sitting on the table. It was orange with a green top. It was like nothing she had ever seen. She went over to smell it. It smelled good! She took a bite. The outside was hard, but the inside was delicious. Soon she had her whole head in the pumpkin. The calves just watched their mother at first. They didn't know if this orange thing would be good to eat but once their mom started eating it, they took a bite too. Soon all three moose were munching on pumpkins.

Mike was eating breakfast when he heard a loud crash outside. There was so much noise that he was almost afraid to look out the window. Finally getting up his courage, he looked outside and saw the funniest sight he had ever seen. Looking at him was Molly and her two calves. Their noses were covered with pumpkin seeds. As soon as they saw that it was only Mike, they went back to eating the pumpkins.

"Everybody come look at this!" Mike cried. Chris, Mom and Dad came to the window. They all started laughing.

"Well, I guess Moose do Trick or Treat." said Mom.. "Their Treat is a real Trick on us!"

"Very funny," said Chris, and they all laughed again at the sight of the three moose with pumpkin seeds all over their faces.

By Bob O'Neil

Roads and Highways

Roads as obstacles: Roadways are home to cars, those large, erratic metal beasts that kill on contact and pose a particular problem for wildlife. Roads epitomize the clash between mechanized civilization and wildlife. Automobiles are the largest single cause of death for wildlife.

Like fences (*See Fences, p. 32*), roads extend for great distances and inevitably cross a migration path or traverse a patch of ideal wildlife habitat. Most wild animals treat roads as clearings in the natural vegetation, either ignoring the cars and moving innocently across, or recognizing the danger and moving cautiously but not having the capacity to understand the rules of the road.

Tolerance of the ubiquitous automobile by wild animals is an indication of their adaptability, but roads and cars are not predictable enough for animals to develop habits for negotiating traffic. Many species of wildlife can be approached by an automobile, merely watching until it stops and people get out or roll down a window. Most of us have noticed how some wild animals will stand calmly by the roadside, waiting. Wildlife cannot be counted on to react to an automobile as we would expect. Horns and lights that would alert domestic dogs and cats to danger tend only to freeze wildlife or to send them running the wrong direction.

Some people have reported that deer whistles, those little devices that attach to the front bumper of a car and emit a high pitched sound inaudible to humans, will alert deer to their presence. For most devices, the car must be travelling over thirty miles per hour to produce a sound. Their effectiveness in actually getting the deer to move from the roadway is difficult to prove, but installing the inexpensive whistles certainly can't hurt.

In addition to the dangers of cars and trucks, road systems often include steep drainage ditches, fences, cattle guards, and bridges. All of these are impediments to the migration and movement of wildlife, and all are danger spots where animals can be expected to mill about indecisively while traffic roars by.

ROADS AS TRAILS: If you could examine an unplowed roadway after a winter night you would find not only the tracks of animals crossing the road, but many trails would come out of the woods, follow the road for a while, and then drop off again. A road makes a great trail, especially late at night when there is little or no traffic and nocturnal animals are about. This activity occurs all year around.

In winter, roads are especially useful to wildlife, providing a snow-free path from one foraging area to another. In a developed area like a wooded subdivision there may be more movement of wildlife on roads than on natural trails. Deer, coyotes, rodents, and porcupines will all use a plowed road to get from one spot to another in deep snow. *(See Bison, p. 61)*

ROADS AS CLEARINGS: Many roads, especially rural access roads and those going into residential developments, are cut through wooded areas. In this case the roadway becomes a clearing in the vegetation where wildlife can take advantage of the open space.

Small birds, rodents and insects that normally hide in vegetation become easy targets for hawks during the day and for owls at night. A mouse seen scurrying across the road may often have a predator close behind. Roads also become gathering places for other birds because insects, gravel, seeds, and puddles of water all attract birds. During unseasonal snowstorms flocks of migrating birds can often be found lingering on the pavement for warmth. Most wild animals using a road for whatever purpose are oblivious to vehicles.

ROADSIDES: Impervious road surfaces like pavement or even hard-packed gravel create zones of green plant growth along their shoulders as they funnel off water.

Roadsides are also an area of perpetual trimming of vegetation which stimulates fresh, new growth that is both tender and nutritious. This is an ideal spot for the growth of weeds and forbs that are good forage for deer. Small herds of migrating deer often stop to feed where they cross a road. In areas using salt or gravel (kept from freezing into lumps by adding salt) to melt road ice, the salt eventually runs off to the shoulders and attracts deer, porcupines, and other animals craving minerals.

WHAT TO DO: Familiarity with your roads and the habitat they pass through helps considerably in anticipating encounters with wildlife. Certain stretches of road along migration routes are traditional crossings and should be approached with care.

Deer seldom travel alone, and the first one to cross is generally leading the group. Once this experienced animal crosses the road the others quickly follow without regard to oncoming cars, so be especially careful if you see a deer that has just crossed ahead of you. Learn to scan the roadsides for deer moving toward the road, and watch at night for the reflection of your headlights in the animals' eyes. Make a mental note when you see an animal that has been hit by a car and remember that spot; slow down when driving through these areas where animals may be present.

On your own property you can cut back vegetation that produces blind spots, avoid using salt on the road, and plow the roads as wide as possible to give animals room to maneuver in winter.

When encountering wildlife on the road in winter, you'll find that animals are reluctant to leave. The plowed-up berms of snow along the sides can be high and hard-packed, or the animal may be too frightened to escape. At night, with blinding headlights in their eyes, animals are even less eager to move.

To help them leave with the least amount of stress, slow down or stop and let the animal pick an exit. If it refuses to leave, proceed slowly to encourage it or try to pass slowly if it moves to one side. Be ready to stop while passing since moose or deer will often jump back in front of a car. Some people have had luck turning off bright headlights for a moment, using only parking lights to alert other motorists. Obviously, this should be done only on deserted or private roads. Alternate use of high and low beams can sometimes stimulate the animals to leave the road.

Since the inception of winter road maintenance for oversnow vehicles in Yellowstone National Park, bison numbers have increased, partly due to the ease of travel. Once restricted in their foraging by deep snow, the bison began using packed roadways to move from one place to another, enabling more animals to survive the winter. Now it is not uncommon to see lines of bison plodding along the roads from one meadow to another. The road system even allows the slow-moving bison, once trapped in the Park, to move out to lower elevations in winter, which unfortunately brings them out of the protection of the Park and into contact with residences and ranches. (See Brucellosis, p. 63)

CHAPTER THREE

Deer

Deer are the most obvious and recognizable animal affected by expanding development into wildlife habitat. They are large, numerous and become quite tame. Deer are adaptable and, if they aren't disturbed, will happily winter in a suburban neighborhood.

Local deer populations can increase dramatically with just a few years of mild winters. Hunting and natural predation usually stop as development occurs in deer habitat, helping to increase the populations even as the available habitat shrinks. Meanwhile, winter becomes a more critical season to deer as their habitat decreases, since that is the time when food is already limited by snowcover and travel is restricted. In response, deer find their way to places where snow is not so deep and winter browse is more plentiful. Residential development in these traditional wintering places, in the foothills and on open southern faces, causes the most conflict.

MULE DEER: Mule deer live in the foothills, mountains, and forest edges of the West. Their stocky bodies and large ears identify them from white-tailed deer, and they are commonly found in and around developed areas. Mule deer migrate up and down the mountains with seasonal snow levels, and in less wintry areas they tend to gather in small herds where they find preferred vegetation. During

MULE DEER
RANGE
Odocoileus hemionus

the summer months older bucks migrate high into the mountains. In heavy snow years mule deer may form "deer yards" where herds of up to a hundred or more gather. Trails will be packed down between areas of browse.

Mule deer are most active in the mornings and evenings and on bright nights. They travel daily up and down hillsides and buttes, and they cross valleys and fields to find food and water. Their routes are usually well established and their behavior predictable, making it easier to anticipate their presence on roads and at fences. They feed mostly on browse: the leaves, shoots, and twigs of shrubs and small trees. In spring and summer they also feed on fresh grass and shoots, mushrooms, and fruit. The mating season runs through the fall, and in the spring one or two spotted fawns will be born to the breeding does.

WHITE-TAILED DEER: Mule deer are more numerous in the mountainous region covered by this book, but white-tailed deer are scattered throughout the area and are locally abundant. White-tailed deer prefer riparian zones, deciduous forests, and the associated fields and farmlands usually found at lower elevations. Their seasonal migrations up and down mountains aren't as extreme as those of the mule deer, but they do respond to winter by moving to areas of less snow. Like mule deer, white-tails will gather into deer yards during severe winters and often end up around homes on lawns and in driveways. They are subject to the same winter stresses and food requirements as mule deer and should be treated the same.

DEER ON THE PROPERTY: A deer is usually a welcome sight near your house; it signifies a closeness to unspoiled land and a live-and-let-live way of life. During the spring and summer young bucks and does with fawns may stay in the lowlands near civilization while the older bucks migrate back up into higher country. This time of year the only conflict with deer usually concerns dogs chasing and killing fawns. Deer are generally healthy because food is plentiful.

The major spring or summer conflict with deer occurs in flower and vegetable gardens, where deer may consume or trample large areas during the evening and night. Succulent forbs and flowers are especially nutritious and are sought in spring by females with nursing young. Spring and summer is also tick season, and extra care should be taken to watch for deer ticks if you are out in gardens or brush where deer have been congregating. *(See Ticks, p. 66)*

WHITETAIL DEER
RANGE
Odocoilus virginianus

With the onset of winter, mule deer begin their descent from the mountains to areas of less snowpack. There are traditional wintering grounds where deer gather, usually on open, windswept hillsides where the vegetation is exposed. From these spots they make daily movements when they need to find additional forage.

People tend to like the same kinds of places as deer: sunny, southern slopes in the foothills, with lots of native trees and shrubs. Snow depth strongly influences deer habits in the winter. Any spot without snow not only reveals forage, but the accompanying ease of travel and movement greatly reduces the energy output required to survive.

Civilization offers several of the easiest places for deer to winter. Houses and other buildings deflect wind and blowing snow, creating pockets of snow-free ground around them. A yard may thus offer not only a place to walk and conserve energy, but there are usually some nutritious shrubs planted conveniently nearby. Winter is a time for energy conservation, so once the deer find a snow-free area with landscaped forage they will settle in. If they are given handouts as well, they will never leave. The younger deer, who are weaker and less experienced, are more often found in civilization. In an area of plentiful deer it's not uncommon to find a handful of yearling deer napping contentedly, nestled up against the warm south-facing wall of a house.

Winter moves mule deer to open hillsides at lower elevations, where they often come into contact with civilization.

Deer are large, numerous and become quite tame. Handouts are inadequate for their needs, often leading to chronic digestive problems and eventual death.

Domestic dogs are a significant problem for wintering deer. Just because your old dog "could never catch a deer" doesn't mean it isn't harming the deer *(See Pets, p.64)*. Any time a dog chases or even disturbs a deer, it causes physical stress, often resulting in death. Many times a deer that appears to escape unharmed will run off, only to lie down from exhaustion and die within a day or two.

DEER AND FENCES: Plowed driveways, roads, and walkways all give deer an easier path to walk in winter, and often draw deer into fenced areas. Fences can be a frequent obstacle since deer make daily migrations. Fences for livestock containment should be adapted for deer use or replaced with a more negotiable type. All unnecessary fences should be removed. Seasonal "let-downs" in high-use areas are also greatly beneficial to the deer. *(See Fences, p. 32)* Barbed wire fencing, especially at the foot of a hill or along a ditch or stream where the deer have trouble jumping, is one of the hardest on deer.

Deer-proofing a yard is difficult without building a high and continuous fence, so the next best thing

is to make it less appealing for them to be in the yard; a lack of food is a good first step. *(See Landscaping, p. 86.)*

FEEDING DEER: Deer are the most commonly fed large wild animal. Their tameness and beauty make it hard to resist giving them a meal, and most people can't help tossing a bit of hay or a handful of apples to the "starving deer." One thing leads to another, and before the winter is over you have a herd of deer dependent on food that is inadequate for their needs. While a bale of hay may help trapped and starving deer survive for a brief period, and it is a passable supplement to natural forage in severe winters, hay alone will eventually cause deer more problems than it solves. Like the moose, a deer's digestive system is adapted to browse, which gives up soluble components and then passes quickly through. Switching to hay, especially when the animal is weak and starving, only produces chronic digestive problems and eventual death.

SIGNS OF DEER: Members of the deer family don't have upper incisor teeth to bite cleanly through vegetation, so visiting deer will leave tell-tale splintered twigs and branches where the vegetation was pulled off. Snow will be pawed away around shrubs to get at grass underneath, and there will be small piles of roundish fecal pellets.

DEER AND LANDSCAPING: Deer prefer to browse on the twigs, leaves, and shoots of shrubs and small trees. In the winter, when they are most likely to come around landscaped areas, they will eat almost anything resembling shrubs, paw for dead grass, and gnaw the bark from trees. They won't eat spruce or pine unless starving and dislike junipers, hawthorne, and a host of other shrubs. *(See Landscaping, p. 86)* Willows and aspens, both native species, are browsed especially hard in the winter.

ENCOURAGING DEER: Deer should be encouraged only in rural areas away from roads, dogs, and other elements of civilization. Keep dogs in control and try to keep all disturbances such as walks with pets, loud machinery, and lights in a predictable pattern. Planting edible natural vegetation in an area where deer winter is the best way to attract them. Browse and forbs (weedy, non-grass plants like vines or flowers) can be utilized each year and will respond to moderate browsing.

DISCOURAGING DEER: Planting unpalatable shrubs and clearing out some of the more heavily browsed species will help to move deer away from dwellings. There are

Deer prints have a characteristic heart shape

commercially available repellents that can be applied to vegetation to keep deer from browsing on them, including some organic ones that will not harm other wildlife or plants. A dog confined to the yard on a chain or wire run at varying times of day and night will keep deer away from the house.

Fertilizer on gardens and lawns makes the plants more palatable and more likely to be eaten by deer, so reducing the use of fertilizers may help. Avoid salting roads and walkways in the winter if possible, as deer are attracted to the salt.

Once deer find a good source of food they will be reluctant to leave, and you may have to get creative to discourage them. There is a wealth of experience in dealing with hungry deer, especially around farms and ranches and long-established homes. Ask around. Water sprayed from a hose is a harmless repellent, and has been used in conjunction with timers and motion sensors. Unpredictable lights and noise usually work, too.

One old fashioned method used to keep deer out of gardens and yards is to place a bar of soap in a cheesecloth bag and hang it from a tree limb. Reportedly, several of these, or bars of soap on sticks, will keep deer away. Apparently they dislike the odor of animal fat or lye in the soap. (*See Landscaping, p. 86*)

Vegetation disliked by Deer

	TREE	FLOWER	SHRUB
Boxelder Maple (*Acer negundo*)			
Columbine (*Aquilegia* sp.)		▓	
Basin Sagebrush (*Artemisia tridentata*)			▓
Pot Marigold (*Calendula officinalis*)		▓	
Scotch Broom (*Cytissus scoparius*)			▓
Dryad (*Dryas hookeriana*)		▓	
Ferns			
English Ivy (*Hedera helix*)			
Iris (*Iris* sp.)		▓	
Juniper (*Juniperus* sp.)			▓
Prickly Phlox (*Leptodactyloon californicum*)		▓	
Lupine (*Lupinus* sp.)		▓	
Daffodil, Narcissus (*Narcissus* sp.)		▓	
Colorado Blue Spruce (*Picea pungens*)	▓		
Ponderosa Pine (*Pinus contorta*)	▓		
Mugho Pine (*Pinus mugho*)	▓		
Ponderosa Pine (*Pinus ponderosa*)	▓		
Limber Pine (*Pinus flexilis*)	▓		
Rosemary (*Rosmarinus officinalis*)			▓
Red Elderberry (*Sambucus racemosa*)			▓
Common Lilac (*Syringa vulgaris*)			▓
Zinnia sp.		▓	
Tulip (*Tulipa* sp.)		▓	

Artificial Feeding

Artificial or supplemental feeding of wildlife is a controversial issue. There are so many variables to consider, such as the species, climate, vegetation, and degree of urgency that each case requires a slightly different strategy. Biologists and wildlife professionals generally discourage feeding on the basis that

although it is well-intentioned it usually causes more problems than it solves. The main concerns are the quality of feed and the problems associated with having wildlife in close proximity to roads, dogs, and the hazards of civilization. In addition, artificially concentrating herds of animals greatly increases the spread of disease and parasites. It often leads to a more dramatic population crash in another year when many weak or sick animals that would normally die may survive to build up large herds containing unhealthy animals.

Continued use of a wintering ground as a feeding station for large numbers of wildlife will degrade the natural vegetation as the animals eat all the wild forage in addition to the supplemental food. Once an area becomes heavily trampled and disturbed it is often invaded by noxious weeds that overwhelm the remaining natural vegetation and compound the problem. (See Landscaping, p. 86)

MAMMALS: You may ask, "Why does the government feed thousands of elk in places like the National Elk Refuge in Jackson Hole, WY, yet they discourage me from feeding a handful of deer in my backyard?" Most biologists agree that supplemental feed for wildlife, even on a closely moni-

tored refuge with a carefully designed diet, is a second-choice situation. They would prefer the animals eat native vegetation and reach a natural population level. The need for feeding arose from the steady encroachment of civilization into traditional wintering grounds essential to wildlife. What occurred with the Jackson Hole elk herd (See Sidebar on p. 17) in the early 1900s continues today with smaller herds of elk, deer, mountain sheep, and moose. Each new residential development takes another bite out of existing habitat for wildlife; each fence re-directs migration; each road kills individual animals; every manicured lawn and golf course uproots native vegetation and sends deer and moose wandering through yards in search of forage.

At some critical point it becomes necessary to decide which is more important: wildlife or ornamental surroundings. A balance can be reached, giving us homesites and providing wildlife with their own corridors and spaces. In this ideal scenario everyone would plant only native vegetation, fences and dogs wouldn't hinder animals as they moved about, and the populations would adjust to fit the available resources. Having to feed deer and moose to keep them from starving in our yards is an indication of a larger problem.

Feeding animals is either unnecessary or it comes when the animals are beyond help. Deer, for example, live most of the year on a diet of browse and forbs. Their digestive systems have evolved and adapted to this vegetation, with adjustments during lean and lush times. Giving them hay, grain, fruit, or other human foods all winter not only causes immediate nutritional problems but makes it difficult for them to return to native plants in the spring. Once the deer are starving they are unable to digest hay at all and will die with full stomachs. Moose are also primarily browsers and unable to subsist on hay; it stays in the digestive system too long and chronic indigestion kills them. Deer, moose, and elk each have a different digestive process that balances the time food digests in the rumen with the time it takes to pass through the system. Deer and moose eat a high volume of browse, which gives up its soluble nutrients quickly and passes on through. Domestic animals, such as cattle, are used to eating poor quality roughage like hay and retaining it long enough to digest it. Elk graze more than they browse so they can adapt readily to alfalfa hay, while deer subsist on supplemental food by picking the choice parts of alfalfa. Elk with access to haystacks have been observed eating only the choice alfalfa heads and leaving the stems.

Moose will survive on a strict hay diet only if they are young and the feeding is continual. Last-minute efforts to save starving moose with hay are fatal. Hay as a supplement on a ranch where moose show up at feeding time is probably not too harmful as long as they are getting enough natural browse as well.

Ted Hartgrave and his ultimate bird, squirrel, weasel and marten feeder.

BIRDS: Nearly everyone feeds birds but feeding birds has the same effect as feeding mammals on a smaller and less noticeable scale. Most birds that visit feeders are seed-eaters, and the supplemental food is very similar to their natural food. Birds are also fed traditionally throughout the winter season, giving them a chance to adjust to the diet before stressful conditions develop, and many are migrating transient birds. Birds are not confined in winter and may fly in from a distance to feed, keeping the population spread out to more natural proportions.

But birds also suffer from being fed; it just isn't as obvious. While a deer killed from starvation in your yard is hard to miss, a dozen songbirds can die and you will never see them. Birds die from predation (cats, hawks) and from flying into windows. They are hit by cars, electrocuted by power lines, suffer diseases and accidents. Any artificial gathering of birds increases the chances something will happen to them.

As with any other kind of animal feeding area, cleanliness will prevent the spread of disease. Periodic scrubbing of bird feeders with bleach and thorough rinsing will eliminate any bacterial and fungal diseases that may develop. A bird feeder is a commitment to provide that service all winter, so make arrangements for someone to stock and clean the feeder when you are away.

This applies to waterfowl as well. Feeding ducks and geese can concentrate large numbers of birds on a small body of water, bringing problems like habitat degradation, disease, and the disruption of breeding cycles. Most biologists discourage feeding waterfowl.

Providing food for hummingbirds in summer is another

(See Birds p. 46), but it also creates artificially high populations that are more prone to accident, disease, and predation. A common sentiment, however, is that feeding and increasing bird numbers only begins to offset the results of pollution, pesticides, and habitat loss. Most people accept bird feeding as a beneficial activity, and the harmful effects are probably offset by the benefits. A lifelong appreciation of wildlife often begins with a simple bird feeder.

Natural Food Sources for Birds	TREE	SHRUB
Serviceberry (*Amelancher arborea*)		
Barberry (*Berberis* spp.)		
Hackberry (*Celtis occidentalis*)		
Crabapple (*Malus* spp.)		
Silverberry (*Elaeagnus commutata*)		
Western Sandcherry (*Prunus besseye*)		
Chokecherry (*Prunus serotina*)		
Skunkbush Sumac (*Rhus trilobata*)		
Currant and Gooseberry (*Ribes* spp.)		
Silver Buffaloberry (*Sheherdia argentea*)		
Snowberry (*Symphoricarpos alba*)		

From Wyoming Game and Fish Dept, 1988, "Wildscape"

The Ant and The Hummingbird

After passing our hummingbird feeder a few times, I noticed that one calliope hummingbird was quite fond of a particular perch. In fact, on closer examination, I found that he was stuck on the feeder! The poor thing was exhausted from fluttering and going nowhere.

Upon inspection, I determined that his beak was stuck inside the feeder hole. I carefully removed the feeder (with calliope attached) from its hook, set it down and watched the poor fellow try to pull his beak out–with no luck.

What in the world? I was stumped. Is his beak broken? Is the plastic cracked? I used a soft cloth to cushion my fingers as I ever so carefully tugged at the thin, tiny, frail bird. No luck. After a deep breath, I tugged again, and pop! Out came bird with beak intact, and one huge carpenter ant speared to the tip of its beak! To my amazement and relief, the bird (with affixed ant) took off! The ant was almost as big as the bird! Apparently, ants got into the sugar water feeder and as the hummingbird inserted its beak for a drink, he also speared an ant. I hope that little bird was able to free his unwitting companion.

By Cathy Fonatsch

(Note: Applying vegetable oil or margarine to the wire that attaches the feeder to the house will keep the ants out of a hummingbird feeder.)

A feed truck distributing pellets as supplemental feed for elk on the National Elk Refuge in Jackson Hole, Wyoming.

THE NATIONAL ELK REFUGE IN JACKSON HOLE, Wyoming is a large-scale example of the problems associated with feeding wildlife. Although the public generally views the refuge as an ideal situation, the biologists who manage and feed the elk don't necessarily profess it to be the best thing to do. Taking over a process of nature, such as providing food and shelter for thousands of elk, is not easy. Over its eighty year history the refuge has evolved from a simple feedlot operation to a complex habitat-management situation.

The refuge was started in response to large numbers of starving elk in the late 1800s and early 1900s, a consequence of severe winters combined with ranchers settling on traditional elk wintering grounds. During the summer, livestock herds grazed the native vegetation that was previously available to the elk through the winter months, so when the elk arrived with winter they were forced to raid ranchers' haystacks to survive.

The initial action was to lure the elk away from the ranches by providing hay. Congress appropriated funds in 1911 to buy hay for the elk, and the following year money began to flow for purchasing land. The basic idea worked, in that the elk began to concentrate on refuge lands. However, the elk recognized a good thing and began to arrive early and stay late, even in mild winters. Elk that normally wintered nearby in isolated herds also gathered on the refuge land. The early refuge managers immediately realized that the key was providing more land, not more hay.

Through various actions the refuge eventually increased to its present size of almost 25,000 acres.

This sounds like a lot of land, but it is estimated to be only twenty-five percent of the historic elk wintering grounds in the Jackson Hole valley. One of the great benefits derived from the entire refuge history was the cooperative effort for habitat preservation made by the involved agencies and organizations.

What began as a simple desire to prevent the elk from starving snowballed into a large, bureaucratic machine that requires constant management changes. The refuge personnel must contend with such varied factors as the biological needs of the elk, fluctuating populations, weather changes, feed costs, habitat conditions, public sentiment, political pressure, and elk diseases, as well as managing other wildlife on the refuge lands. Since 1943, fall hunting of elk by private citizens has been used to help control herd numbers and to scatter the early migrants onto adjacent federal lands.

Although supplemental food is given to the elk only to prevent damage to the natural vegetation or when the snow becomes too deep, the public perception of the refuge is still that it is a winter-long feedground. In 1975 baled hay was replaced with pelletized alfalfa, a less wasteful form of food.

Despite all its problems, the elk refuge is remarkably successful as both a winter haven for elk and as a land preserve. Still, the refuge managers, when asked how to go about starting a feeding program for displaced wildlife, recommend against feeding just to maintain animal numbers. The lesson the refuge offers is that habitat is the crucial element, and that once you begin feeding animals in place of the natural vegetation of that habitat, you can't stop.

Uncle Bert Raynes' Advice on Birds

We do what we can to keep birds from being accidentally killed or injured on the windows of our home.

Any window can become reflective, become a mirror, at some particular moment during the day depending on the pane's orientation, on atmospheric conditions, even its cleanliness. A bird can so easily be deceived into believing it's flying into open, safe space and crash into the glass. It may be killed outright, seriously injured or simply stunned and thus easy pickings for predators.

In spring and fall migrations, birds unfamiliar with the local terrain are particularly vulnerable to window strikes. Young birds, unfamiliar with their world, are also subject to confusion about where to fly. Accidents happen all year long, but the peak periods are the migrations.

The toll is staggering. Birds by the tens of millions die each year during migrations just in the United States. Two hazards alone, windows and domestic cats, together are responsible for the deaths of millions upon millions of birds yearly, mostly songbirds, but almost no species seems invulnerable. However, some precautions humans can, and should, take will reduce the slaughter.

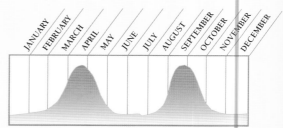

BIRD MIGRATION PERIODS

So, we do what we can. First, we don't have a cat; if we did it would be a house cat. Period. Then, during bird migration periods we place lamps with low

Clark's nutcracker at feeder. Hanging objects help alert birds of windows.

wattage bulbs, 40 watts or greater, in appropriate windows, those windows with any history of having birds fly into them. We simply keep them on during all daylight hours, dawn to dusk, for the couple of weeks of migration.

Other homeowners and building managers attach falcon silhouettes to their problem windows; some have windsocks or similar dangling, easily removed signals to alert birds to imminent danger; a few people go so far as to put netting up a few inches from and over even picture windows(!); and we're experimenting with a hint that Post-Its, easily removable, no-staining note papers on window surfaces will warn birds off. We try about any idea out; a bird saved is worth the small effort involved.

We have avoided any window treatment such as glare reducing films which enhance the mirror effect of the glass. And some, ahem, eschew too rigorous window cleaning, particularly during the brief migration periods.

Well, now. All that consideration, all your good works, and yet a bird has hit a window. It lies on the ground, panting, alive but twisted or sprawling, on its back. What to do? First, approach the victim slowly; birds fear humans, with good reason. The bird may right itself and flutter off. A hopeful sign.

Second, if the bird seems unable to move, slowly again, gently place it on its keel, or on one side, and retreat. It may recover in a matter of some minutes.

Third, since a bird in an awkward position and unable to fly is a target for predators, feathered or furred, carefully and gently—do NOT squeeze—place the bird into a cardboard box with holes poked in the top and at least one side, or a large paper bag with the top loosely closed. Put it in the shade, out of the wind, in a safe place. Most birds that hit windows are diurnal and will rest or sleep in the dim or dark confines of a box or paper bag. A slight build-up of carbon dioxide in their immediate atmosphere is often helpful as well. Of course, if they die there, the end is more peaceful.

Fine; after a half hour or hour make an inspection. If all is well, the bird will react to light by attempting to escape, fluttering its wings, scratching at the container. Wonderful. Let it go.

If not, it gets dicey. Strict federal and state laws apply to the possession of wild birds, alive or dead. Two exceptions are house sparrows and starlings. Compassion usually wins out. If you know the bird species, it will help you in its temporary care. You will know what the bird eats in the wild and will provide a reasonable substitute. If you don't know, check the bird's beak to see if it appears to be a seed eater (strong, curved bill), an insect eater (pointed, slim), or meat eater(hooked). NOT every bird will eat worms or bugs; NOT every species can eat seeds. All may drink water; provide it in a large, quite shallow dish. Seek professional or experienced help. Do keep in mind that the odds are very much against an injured bird's recovery. Against you.

But. If it all works and a bird recovers to fly away on strong wings, you will feel really good. A promise.

By Bert Raynes, author of The Birds of Grand Teton National Park.
Bert is a long-time resident of Jackson Hole, and writes a weekly column about Jackson's bird life in the Jackson Hole News. His latest book is Valley so Sweet.

elk fawn

Elk

Elk, large members of the deer family, are now found mostly in the western United States. They live in groups ranging in size from ten to twenty animals in the forest and to herds of several hundred in open country. Cow elk lead the herds except during the mating season when bulls defend and control bands of females.

Elk are primarily grazers, pawing through the snow in winter and feeding on fresh grass in the spring and summer. In winter, or other times when food is scarce, they browse like other deer, eat lichens and moss, and gnaw tree bark. They are most active at night, feeding and moving from dusk to dawn.

The breeding season occurs in the fall, and calves are born in late spring or early summer in traditional calving areas, usually on the way from wintering grounds to summer range.

Elk gather for fall migration out of the high country and winter on traditional grounds in large herds. They travel mostly at night, with the cows and calves calling to each other. After the mating season, when migration begins, bulls separate from the others and join into small groups. Cows, calves, and young bulls stay together.

Elk herds establish migration routes between winter and summer ranges, but the arrival of residential and agricultural development has broken up most wintering grounds and diverted the elk from traditional migration trails. Often elk find themselves traveling through residential developments and wintering in backyards. Elk prefer to winter in lower meadows and thickly forested hillsides where they can paw through the snow to find grass. They often end up along rivers and streams where summer growth is most plentiful.

ELK ON YOUR PROPERTY: A few elk live year-round in the lower country, especially in wooded areas along rivers or streams and in larger protected tracts. For the most part, elk in residential areas will be winter residents only or simply migrate through. You will quickly learn if you live on a migration route as it may look like a herd of cattle stampeded through: broken fences, trampled vegetation, and a wide trail of tracks tear across the land. The best thing you can do is to lower or remove sections of fence ahead of time to let the elk pass. *(See Fences, p. 32)*

ELK
RANGE
Cervus elaphus

Elk migrate mostly at night and often during a big snowstorm, so barbed wire and other wire fences are especially difficult for them. It isn't uncommon to hear the stretching and breaking of a wire fence mingled with the calls of cows and calves as an elk herd passes through, and daylight often finds a cow or calf caught by the hind leg and lying exhausted in the snow. Once the lead cow elk gets over a fence the rest will follow in a rush, often running blindly in the middle of the herd, so let-downs and open spaces need to be large enough to let them pass. They won't line up single file to go over a narrow let-down.

If elk are wintering near you on a regular basis you can encourage them by planting native grasses and irrigating existing vegetation so there will be forage available. If you are hosting a number of elk you may get some assistance in the form of advice from state agencies, but most elk on private land involves only small bands or individual animals.

Older bulls especially tend to break away in winter and live alone. Dogs should be restrained and human disturbance minimized. Like all wild animals in winter, elk are often surviving on minimal energy levels and can be easily exhausted if forced to run in snow.

FEEDING ELK: The preferred action is not to feed elk and to let nature take its course. Although it is difficult to see animals in poor condition, artificial feeding tends to build up populations to the point of damage to natural forage and the elk will die off in greater numbers during a hard year.

Because elk are primarily grazers they are able to adapt quickly to a diet of hay, especially if it is supplemental to natural vegetation. They will become conditioned to it, so once started any feeding program must be continued seven days a week until the snow recedes. It should also be started before animals begin to starve. Feeding wild animals is a major commitment of time and resources. The commitment will also grow as more and more elk return each winter.

SIGNS OF ELK: Migrating elk leave a wide swath, from downed fences to trampled vegetation. Cows and calves call to each other in what sounds a bit like air squealing out of a big balloon. Their tracks are large at about four inches long.

At other times of the year elk will strip the bark from tree seedlings and shrubs, bulls will rub bark from trees, thrash small saplings with their antlers during the rut and leave a strong, musky scent in the air. Cows

Winter brings elk out of the high country to form herds on open hillsides.

will leave beds in the grass and grazed vegetation.

ELK AND LANDSCAPING: Elk are less likely to end up in your yard than deer or moose, and their arrival usually means they are close to starving. At this point they will eat whatever is handy, from shrubs to pine trees. If you live close to a regular elk wintering area and they wander into your yard often, you can plant native species that are unpalatable or will withstand browsing. (*See Landscaping, p. 86*)

Loss of winter habitat means elk must concentrate on available land.

ENCOURAGING ELK: Planting food like grasses and forbs and removing fences are about the only things you can do to attract elk. Salt blocks should not be used to attract elk or other wildlife. Supplemental feeding should be done only as a last resort, and with the approval and advice of game officials. States have differing laws concerning the feeding of wildlife, so check before you consider feeding. Some residential developments and home-owner's associations also restrict the feeding of wildlife.

DISCOURAGING ELK: Lack of food, high fences that force them to go around gardens or yards, noise, and light will repel elk. Unless you have the only forage around, elk are more likely to keep moving than are deer or moose. Commercial repellents on vegetation may keep shrubs from being browsed, and a barking dog will discourage elk. Elk may carry the disease brucellosis, (See p. 63), so close contact between elk and livestock during certain times of the year should be avoided.

Poor distribution of feed often leads to elk feeding along with cattle.

Vegetation disliked by Elk

	TREE	FLOWER	SHRUB
Boxelder Maple (*Acer negundo*)			
Englemann Spruce (*Picia* spp.)			
Pines (*Pinus* spp.)			
Larch (*Larix* spp.)			
Honesuckle (*Lonicera* spp.)			■
Smoke Tree (*Cotinus coggygria*)			
Russian Olive (*Elaeagnus angustifolia*)			■
Hawthorne (*Crataegus* spp.)			
Dryad (*Dryas drummondii*)			■
Common Juniper (*Juniperus communis*)			
Raspberry (*Rubus* spp.)			■
Creeping Mahonia (*Mahonia repens*)			
White Spirea (*Spirea lucida*)			■

"Elk Can Swim, Can't They"

The phone rang and I wiped the sleep from my eyes as I answered it. Glancing at the clock, I saw that it was 5:30 in the morning. "Hello."

"Elk can swim can't they?" came the voice from the other end.

Five minutes of confusion followed as I tried to decipher individually who was on the phone with me, why it was important whether elk could swim or not, and most importantly why it couldn't have waited until later in the day. It turned out to be my friend Pat, who lived in a subdivision outside town just against the mountains surrounding Buffalo, Wyoming.

He had just inherited some money and decided to put in a pool. The concrete for the pool had been poured, but he hadn't yet put the fence around his backyard. We had always liked to sit on the back porch at night and watch the elk migrate down to the river. Sometime during the night, a herd must have gone by and tried to cut through the yard because when I got to his house, there was a young bull standing in the middle of his yet waterless pool.

Pat thought that he might be able to fill the pool with water and the elk would be able to swim his way out. An idea with merit, I thought, but maybe a bit too drastic at this point. I said we should just build a wooden ramp, slide it into the pool, and then chase the elk out or draw him out with some hay. We decided to try the latter plan first.

We nailed sheets of plywood onto a couple of six by sixes and slid it into the pool, all the while trying to ignore the ready advice of everyone else, for by this time all of Pat's neighbors were gathered to watch the action. They figured if anyone was going to come up with a dumb scheme to get the elk out of the pool it would be us!

The ramp securely placed in the pool, we decided the humane thing to do would be to try to entice the elk out with hay. It didn't work, I guess he was too scared to be hungry. We figured he might be thirsty, so we tried a bucket of water. It didn't work, I guess he was too scared to be thirsty. Next we tried scaring it out. It didn't work. I guess he was too scared to be....Well, it didn't work anyway.

It was now past ten and everyone agreed it was time to get the professionals involved. Dejectedly, Pat and I walked to the house to call the Game and Fish Department as the rest of the community went back to their houses to get refreshments and more film.

After calling Game and Fish, we each grabbed a beer and looked out the window to see the elk sniffing at the ramp. He took one tentative step onto it, then another, until his entire front end was on it. We both held our breath, anxiously waiting to see if our engineering would hold up and if he would climb out on his own. He backed off the ramp and we figured that the Game and Fish guys would have to hoist him out when the elk stepped to the side of the ramp, and simple as you please, jumped out of the pool onto the lawn and trotted off into the woods, head held high.

Everyone, including the Game and Fish biologists, were disappointed to find that the elk was gone. Pat and I were disappointed that the elk didn't have the common courtesy to use the ramp we had made for him.

By Kevin Ruddleyer

Mice, Pocket Gophers, Ground Squirrels, and Squirrels

Rodents likely to occur around homes and developments range from subterranean pocket gophers, which seldom peer above ground, to tree squirrels living forty feet above the ground. Mice are the most common rodent visitor. Homeowners' concerns with these rodents revolve mostly around decreasing

their numbers and keeping them from damaging property. Rodents are also a concern because they carry several human diseases. *(See Diseases, p. 66)* Rodents, although considered pests, are a major food source for predators like owls, hawks, coyotes, and weasels.

MICE: Deer mice are the most common uninvited houseguest and are the model for cartoon mice with their big, dark eyes, large ears, and soft fur. Deer mice are mostly nocturnal and feed on seeds, nuts, fruit, insects, vegetation, and carrion. In a domestic situation they eat anything, gnawing into bags and boxes and nibbling on butter, fruit and bread. In the wild, deer mice build nests of chewed up plant fiber, but once inside a house they use insulation, paper, cloth, or any other accessible material. They can crawl through a surprisingly small opening, and have been known to find their way into stove insulation, electrical controls, and exposed wiring inside water heaters. Deer mice are also carriers of the hantavirus, a deadly virus limited mostly to the Southwest. *(See Diseases p. 66)*

The heavy bodied vole, referred to as a "field mouse," is found outside the house, on porches, in garages and barns, and particularly on the ground under boards and piles of cuttings. At first glance these dark mice are almost featureless with only tiny eyes at one end and a tail at the other to tell you which is which. They feed largely on seeds and shoots of vegetation and seldom venture indoors. Voles are responsible for the little mounds of grass and long, snaking trails of clipped grass laced across your yard when the snow melts. In winter, voles will gnaw the bark off sapling trees below the snowline at ground level. Protect new plantings by wrapping the trunks with metal flashing.

Mouse populations are large and their potential for breeding tremendous. They are held in check only by predators and the limitations of their food. Encouraging natural predators helps reduce populations; ermine, weasels, hawks, and owls all prey on mice and may take up residence around dwellings if not disturbed. Domestic cats are great mousers and will keep a building mouse-free, but they are deadly to songbirds. Mouse traps work indoors for specific sites; snap traps are designed to kill instantly, or live traps may be used and the mice taken to a remote location and released. However, while releasing mice in a new location may make you feel better, it may

Golden-mantled Ground Squirrel

only be a delayed death sentence for the mouse; the chances are good that the mouse will die or be eaten by predators in unfamiliar surroundings.

The ideal solution is to mouse-proof all buildings and let the outdoors take care of itself. Mice are amazingly adept at getting through small cracks around building foundations, eaves, pipes and wires, and under loose siding. You should caulk or screen every opening greater than a quarter-inch.

POCKET GOPHERS: The seldom-seen pocket gopher is responsible for the mounds of fresh dirt found on your lawn or garden in the morning and for the wormlike dirt tubes, or eskers, lying on the ground in spring after the snow melts. Pocket gophers do not hibernate and often burrow up through the snow, then close up the snow tunnels with soil from below. These long plugs end up on the ground when the snow melts.

Pocket gophers are named for the big external pouches, or pockets, in their cheeks where they carry food and nesting material. They feed mostly on roots, grass, and green shoots, which they may pull down into their tunnels and cache in a storeroom. They do particular damage to gardens and young trees and may chew on underground pipes and wires.

Pocket gophers are beneficial to the overall natural condition of an area. Their extensive burrows help aerate and enrich the soil and increase moisture percolation. Old gopher burrows are used by many other animals. A gopher burrow may have hundreds of feet of tunnels with separate rooms for sleeping, food storage, and defecation. Gophers move as easily backward through their tunnels as they do forward. Gophers are preyed upon by badgers, coyotes, and other digging predators, as well as snakes and weasels.

POCKET GOPHER
RANGE

Thomomys talpoides

Pocket gophers can be kept out of a yard or garden by burying a wire mesh fence (quarter-inch mesh) at least eighteen to twenty inches deep. Gophers already in a yard or garden can be easily trapped by exposing one of their tunnels to daylight. Use a metal probe or dowel near a fresh dirt mound to find the tunnel, then dig with a shovel to expose a section of tunnel. A trap, either to catch the gopher alive or to kill it, can be set in the exposed tunnel.

Flooding tunnels with water or using noxious gas seldom works because of the extent of the gophers' tunnels, and poisons may affect other animals as well. In the long-running battle with pocket gophers, people have tried everything from ferrets to automobile exhaust. There are alternatives such as devices that emit vibrations or ultrasonic sounds to discourage gophers.

A persistent and wary gopher can be especially irksome. In her book "Old Jules," about the harsh life of a Nebraska homesteader in the 1800s, Mari Sandoz describes how the frustrated farmer battled one annoying gopher. Jules, who didn't have a moment of leisure in his hard life, spent nearly half a day lying in the garden with the barrel of his shotgun buried in the gopher's tunnel. He was waiting to pull the trigger when he saw the gopher move the little pile of dirt in front of the shotgun.

GROUND SQUIRRELS: Often called "gophers" by mistake, ground squirrels are burrowing rodents but may reside in rock piles, wood piles, or under porches and foundations. There are several species of ground squirrels: some are striped, spotted, and some have no distinct markings. Check a local field guide for positive identification. Ground squirrels hibernate as much as six months of the year, so the remaining time is spent breeding, raising young, and eating. Most ground squirrels are diurnal. They feed on grass shoots and most other vegetation, occasionally insects and carrion. The Uinta ground squirrel, for example, is often seen on highways feeding on another Uinta hit by a car.

As with other rodents, ground squirrels in reasonable and natural numbers can be beneficial. They adapt easily to the presence of humans and can be fun to observe. The more numerous they are, however, the more damage they can do. Vegetable and flower gardens are often hard hit, as well as lawns, tree shoots, and shrubs. Pipes, wires, and wood siding can be chewed up. Their burrows become extensive and spread across a lawn or pasture, and the openings can be a hazard to horses and livestock.

Uinta Ground Squirrel

severe problem you are better off protecting gardens and flower beds for the short period the rodents are out. Generally it is the availability of food and the lack of natural predators found in a residential setting that leads

UINTA GROUND
SQUIRREL RANGE
Spermophilus armatus

to large numbers of ground squirrels. They are also numerous in areas of disturbed soil like hayfields, along roadways and in yards where the growth of new grass and weeds is abundant. Ground squirrels and their habits may be annoying, but battling them can be a frustrating experience. People who have stopped their efforts to control ground squirrel numbers report the subsequent arrival of a fascinating array of predators: hawks, coyotes, badgers, and owls. One ground squirrel colony even attracted a great blue heron, which would stand motionlessly by a burrow entrance to spear emerging rodents and swallow them whole.

TREE SQUIRRELS: The red squirrel and gray squirrel are the most common tree squirrels and adapt readily to human presence. Both species are tolerant of a certain amount of activity, and often inhabit attics, eaves and barns. They are notorious raiders of bird feeders. In addition, the fox squirrel is an eastern species that is found in a few lower elevations in the west and requires deciduous trees. The bright, chattering red squirrel is common in pine and spruce forests of the west where it feeds on buds and seeds, scattering the husks of pine cones on the ground below. Red squirrels nest in hollows or leaf nests and store their collection of seeds in built-up piles beneath the trees. They are active all winter, tunneling through the snow to reach their food caches.

Red squirrels often find their way into attics through ventilation holes, old woodpecker holes or under loose boards. They will chew and enlarge a small opening until they can fit through. They appropriate this space and use it as a tree hollow, building a nest and raising young and storing food. Squirrels can be noisy, messy guests and can damage electrical wiring as well as chewing window and door trim. Squirrels are most damaging if they clamber in through a chimney or open window and can't find a way out, chewing at everything in an attempt to escape.

Red squirrels are territorial and only breed once a year, so there usually isn't a problem with hordes of squirrels

Ground squirrels are difficult to exclude from a property and most means of control involve killing the animals. They can be easily live-trapped and removed if there are only a few animals. Cats and some breeds of dogs are effective at keeping numbers down. Unless you have a

NOTE:
If you have a large, open container of water, such as a barrel or horse trough, you can provide an avenue of escape for squirrels or other small animals that may fall in. A branch or board fastened to the rim and sloping into the water works well.

RED SQUIRREL
RANGE

Tamiasciurus hudsonicus

N. FLYING SQUIRREL
RANGE

Glaucomys sabrinus

over-running a home. However, several red squirrels can sound and act like a horde. Most situations can be solved by blocking entrances to attics with flashing or mesh and removing any food source such as bird feeders or stores of dried dog food. Bird feeders can be set on a post and metal flashing used around the post. Squirrels can leap incredible distances from a tree or roof to reach a bird feeder, so feeders need to be kept in the clear. Individual squirrels can be live-trapped and moved far away and released, although care should be taken during spring and summer not to trap a female with young hidden away somewhere; after breeding the females defend their own territories without the males, keeping all other squirrels out.

Flying squirrels are a shy, nocturnal type of tree squirrel that have evolved large folds of skin for gliding from one tree to another. They nest in hollows and feed on the ground and in trees. Unless you make a specific night-time search or stumble on a nesting hollow you may never know they are there.

Northern Flying Squirrel

A Rodent Story

Photographer Tom Mangelsen was getting ready to go to the airport to leave on a three-week trip to the arctic. He had his new custom van parked in the driveway with the doors open while he shuttled equipment cases back and forth. It was early summer, and the Uinta ground squirrels were everywhere, sitting on his wood-pile and running across the yard. Tom left them alone during their brief summer, and they were tame and curious. At one point he had to shoo one away from the open door of his van.

Tom was running late as usual and had everything out of the van and stacked in the driveway just in time for his ride to the airport. He closed the door to the van and left it.

When he returned three weeks later and opened up the van he noticed an overpowering smell of animal urine. Then he saw that the carpet was chewed to shreds all around the sliding door. When he opened the front doors he found the trim and carpeting chewed up there as well. Tom realized that he must have trapped a ground squirrel inside when he closed the van door three weeks earlier, and it had tried to chew its way out. He expected to find it dead and smelling somewhere in the van, but the ground squirrel had gnawed at every likely spot to get out and had finally eaten away the rubber boot surrounding the gearshift and crawled out that way. Now Tom never closes the car door without first checking around for squirrels.

C.C.

bushy-tailed woodrat

The Disappearing Garden

Growing a garden in northwestern Wyoming is darn near impossible—a good garden, anyway. But one spring while living in Moose, Wyoming, my husband and I decided to try. And, lo and behold, things grew. The radishes, onions, and lettuce were fine, but the broccoli, Brussels sprouts, and cauliflower were spectacular! We had also planned a fall trip to Europe. The day after Labor Day we loaded our dog and our suitcases in our car and headed East. Before we left, we took a last look at our garden, knowing the frost would kill the plants before we returned in late October. Upon our return, we expected to find withered and dead plants

Imagine our surprise to find the plants—GONE! Small stalks an inch or two high were all that remained of our once bountiful crops. "The neighbors?" my husband Jim asked. I shook my head. "That would be too weird," I replied. We unpacked in a house chilled by the cooler fall weather. Jim went out to the back porch for wood to start a fire. He found our garden—neatly harvested and stacked on top of the cords of wood! "The neighbors?" he asked. "Too weird," I replied.

Before bedtime that night, Jim went to the back porch to get another stick or two of wood. He flipped on the light, then I heard "Well, what the heck is that?" Peering over his shoulder, I saw an animal totally new to both of us: it looked like a rat with a big, bushy tail staring at us from the top row of wood, in the midst of the drying plants. "Wow," I whispered, and dove for the mammal identification books. "Bushy-tailed Woodrat. I'll be darned." And we began learning about a wild animal who had decided that our home

was his home, too. A National Park Service biologist confirmed my identification and advised us not to leave anything shiny and valuable outside," And rightly so—bottle caps disappeared, along with a teaspoon and a new screw and washer. One night we rolled a ball of aluminum foil and left it near the woodpile. It was gone the next morning. A few days later, we left another. The woodrat was completely unafraid of us, and he began to wait expectantly for his shiny "ball." But we only saw him late at night; we had no idea where he spent the daylight hours. Then, one evening in March, he wasn't waiting to play. "Funny, the rat's not out there tonight," Jim remarked, coming in with a load of wood. The next morning, we discovered where he had gone. Across our backyard, coming in a direct line to the back porch, were the up-and-down tunneling tracks of a short-tailed weasel. In his winter white coat, this cunning hunter had discovered the woodrat and taken him, leaving only a small smudge of blood in the snow.

As spring turned to early summer that year, our woodpile disappeared. As I was cleaning out the back porch in preparation for yet another year's wood supply, I found a hidden treasure, shiny in the sunlight: a teaspoon, a screw and washer, some bottle caps, and several foil balls. We've had other gardens and other winters since the year the woodrat lived with us, but bringing in the wood for the night has never been as much fun.

By Linda Olson, Grand Teton National Park, Moose, Wy

CHAPTER SEVEN

Pronghorns

Pronghorns are commonly called antelope because of their resemblance to African antelope species like the gazelle, but the North American pronghorn is alone in this family. They have true horns with a solid, bony core covered with a hornlike sheath. The sheath is comprised of agglutinated hair and is shed each year. Both sexes have horns. Pronghorns are creatures of the grasslands and open prairies and are the fastest animals on the continent. They live in small bands, feeding on browse such as sagebrush and eating forbs and grasses. In peak years bands of pronghorn may gather into herds of a thousand or more.

Pronghorns historically numbered in the millions but paralleled the fate of the bison in the American West. Since the early 1920s they have been steadily increasing and expanding their range.

PRONGHORNS AND PROPERTY: Although pronghorns live in the open western prairies, they migrate between summer and winter ranges and often pass through or near developed areas. They are common on many ranches and often share hayfields with livestock. As they expand their summer limits in years of high populations, bands may get pushed into searching for food, and more and more contact with residential areas is likely. Pronghorns are alert and skittish, although if undisturbed will remain in a hayfield for weeks at a time. Most encounters with pronghorn occur at a distance.

PRONGHORN RANGE

Antilocarpra americana

ENCOURAGING PRONGHORNS: As with many other wildlife species, you either have them or you don't. In an area where pronghorn live, visit seasonally, or just migrate through, you can plant native forbs and grasses and try not to disturb the animals. Fences can be a major obstacle for pronghorn since they prefer to crawl under or through a fence rather than jump over. (*See Fences p. 32*) Fences can be adapted for pronghorns, or sections can be let down seasonally. In heavy snow years pronghorns congregate along highways, railways, and other areas free of snow. Right-of-way fences and long property line fences can inhibit migration and funnel the pronghorns onto roads.

DISCOURAGING PRONGHORNS:
Pronghorns are easily frightened and a few days of disturbance will move them away. However, they are essentially harmless and their feeding doesn't compete with cattle and only somewhat with sheep and horses.

Pronghorn

Meadowlark

Fences

Fences were originally developed to protect the first domestic animals from wild animals. From there fences evolved to become barriers to keep animals both in and out, boundary markers and decoration. Fences have historically been made of the most plentiful materials at hand, such as meandering limestone rock walls

in the eastern U.S. and lodgepole pine buck and rail fences in the West.

The development of wire fencing material, from barbed wire to heavy steel, meshlike fences, greatly increased the possible sizes and lengths of fences. Especially in the West, where vast acreage is necessary to support traditional agricultural practices, fences became status symbols.

Conflicts with wildlife weren't an issue in the Old West because the whole idea was to keep the cattle from having to compete with wildlife. Fences were designed to be barriers for livestock, to keep any animal from passing through, and if a few deer got hung up that was just a bit less competition for the range. There was plenty of room for the wildlife to go somewhere else and not compete with livestock. The end result is that the fences in use today are largely those developed as solid barriers, with no allowances for wildlife.

Mountain Bluebird

When wild animals such as deer or elk encounter a fence they treat it as they would a natural obstacle. They are usually driven by hunger, fear, or migration, and the need to press on is too compelling for them to be turned aside by a fence. Some species of wildlife try to jump over, some crawl under, and some attempt to charge through. If the fence is totally impassable they may panic and exhaust themselves running back and forth or simply following along it, trying to find a way around.

Since wildlife species generally approach a fence differently than domestic animals do, changes in the structure of the fence can be made that will enable the wildlife to pass safely through and still keep the domestic animals contained.

In general, long property fences should be made wildlife-friendly, while smaller enclosures like gardens and yards can be made impassable. Most wild animals

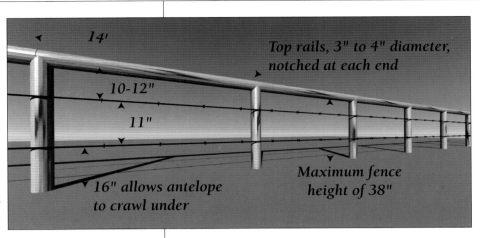

14'

10-12"

11"

Top rails, 3" to 4" diameter, notched at each end

16" allows antelope to crawl under

Maximum fence height of 38"

follow traditonal migration routes, trails, and seasonal or daily paths. Their paths are predictable, and fences can be altered to allow wildlife to pass unharmed. Livestock fences can be designed so that portions can be lowered or opened when livestock control isn't needed. Consider the option of having no fences at all if you are only delineating property lines; you can plant trees to create beautiful boundary markers.

For the most part fences affect only larger animals such as deer, elk, moose, and pronghorn, but fences that cross water, such as a stream or canal, pose a particular threat for large waterfowl, which need long stretches of open

FENCE SPECIFICATIONS FOR ALLOWING WILDLIFE TO PASS

PURPOSE OF FENCE	FENCE SPECIFICATIONS*
Enclose cattle and horses, allow **DEER** to pass	38" w/ 3 to 4 strands of barbed wire, top two strands 10"-12" apart
Enclose cattle and horses, adjacent to highway, allow **DEER** to pass	48"** with 4 strands of barbed wire, with top rail
Enclose sheep, adjacent to highway, allow **DEER** to pass	45" with 5 strands of barbed wire OR 45" with 2 strands of barbed wire over 26" woven wire
Allow **DEER**, **ELK** and **MOOSE** to cross	Barbed wire with let down fence sections OR woven wire with let-down fence sections
Enclose cattle and horses, allow **PRONGHORN** to cross	38" with 3 strands barbed wire, bottom 16" above ground, smooth
Enclose sheep, allow **PRONGHORN** to cross	32" with 4 strands barbed wire, bottom 10" above ground, smooth
Enclose cattle and sheep, allow **PRONGHORN** to cross	38" with 4 strands of barbed wire, bottom 10" above ground, smooth
Allow infrequent crossing of **ELK** and **MOOSE**	38" with 3 strands of barbed wire, bottom 16" above ground
Allow frequent crossing of **ELK** and **MOOSE**	38" with 2 strands of barbed wire, bottom 16" above ground, with top rail
Allow frequent crossing to winter range of **ELK** and **MOOSE**	38" with 3 strands of barbed wire, bottom 10" above ground, with top rail

*Fence specifications from Wyoming Game and Fish Department Habitat Extension Bulletin #53.
**Specifications from Wyoming Department of Transportation specifiy this high of fence when near highways.

Deer jump over a fence by drawing their legs under their bodies as they leap. If one or both hind legs fail to clear the top wire, the legs can become entangled in the top and second wire. The distance between the top two strands of this fence should have been a minimum of 10 inches, preferably 12 inches.

Pronghorn entangled in barbed wire

water to take off and land safely. In particular, swans can be killed by hitting a wire fence while trying to land or take off. Wherever possible, stop a fence at the water's edge rather than cross it.

On the good side, fenceposts in open country like meadows or pastures provide important perches for birds to display, hunt, or rest. Fenceposts are great places for birdhouses, especially for insect-eating species like bluebirds. One possible design is to build low fences with occasional high posts for wildlife use.

BUILDING FENCES TO REDUCE WILDLIFE CONFLICTS:

BARBED WIRE: Barbed wire was designed for containing cattle and is harmful to horses and wildlife. Barbed wire fences are notorious for trapping animals like deer or moose by the hind leg as they try to jump over. If the wires are a bit loose, which is often the case with fences in areas frequented by wildlife or livestock, the animal's hind foot slips between the top two wires and twists them together around the foot as the animal lands. The more the animal struggles the tighter the wire twists, until shock and exhaustion kill it. There are several options to help prevent this, in addition to maintaining a tight fence. One is to place the second wire twelve inches below the top wire to give more room. Another is to use a wooden rail for the top of the fence. Besides eliminating the upper wire, this also makes the fence more visible. Often at night, or when in a panic, animals don't even see a wire fence. Vertical wooden stays can be woven through the wires between fence posts to hold the wires in place and prevent them from twisting.

Since not all animals will attempt to jump over a fence, the bottom wire is also important. Pronghorn and young deer, moose, and elk prefer to crawl under or through a fence. The bottom wire should be unbarbed and should be

Bighorn lining up to cross fence

no closer than sixteen inches from the ground. Stays should be removed to allow the wires to spread slightly if the animals persist in climbing through. The top of all fences should be no more than about forty inches from the ground. Game officials suggest these safer guidelines for all fences, regardless of the wildlife species crossing the fence.

BUCKRAIL: Although a traditional and popular fence, the rustic buckrail is one of the least wildlife friendly fences in use. The design requires a high and wide construction with multiple places to injure or break legs. Traditional buckrail fences are at least forty-eight inches high, almost a foot taller than required for safe wildlife passage. Livestock owners contend that a buckrail fence lower than forty-eight inches won't contain certain stock, so perhaps some other, more negotiable fence type, such as post and rail, should be used for livestock.

The buckrail and other wooden fences are best used as perimeter fences in areas of low wildlife use, or dividing

Buckrail fence with winter let-down

land that is not used heavily by livestock. In migration corridors or other areas frequented by wildlife, the fence can be constructed to have let-down panels or removable sections that are lowered during migration. Again, the top rail of the fence should ideally be no more than forty inches from the ground. The legs of the fence bucks should spread no more than four feet at their base so the fence isn't too wide to jump; having a low fence doesn't help if the animal can't jump far enough to clear all the rails.

POST AND RAIL: This is the preferred fence for wildlife in most cases; it is a good perimeter fence that is easy for wildlife to negotiate. The top rail should be about forty inches above the ground, and the bottom rail should be at least sixteen inches above the ground. Let-down sections can be

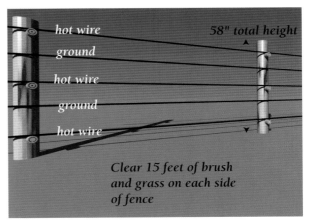

Electric fences

easily incorporated and lowered during the migration months.

ELECTRIC: Electric fences are generally used for smaller areas such as gardens or pastures, and are not likely to cross migration routes, but they should be marked with flags for visibility and kept to the same heights as other fences. They are often overlooked by homeowners as an alternative, low-impact fence.

Electric fences are relatively cheap and easily let down or removed when not needed, and they can be powered by solar panels. Electric fences work especially well for temporarily sectioning off areas. An electric fence is a good choice for handling a seasonally occurring incident, such as deer feeding in planted crops or in yards.

METAL: Metal materials, such as wire mesh, come in various sizes and designs and can be used to prevent specific animals from passing through. They are most useful around gardens and yards to prevent unwanted rodents or small predators from entering, but they should not be used if wildlife passage is desired.

Fences should not be doubled, one functional and one decorative, and adjoining landowners do not each need to

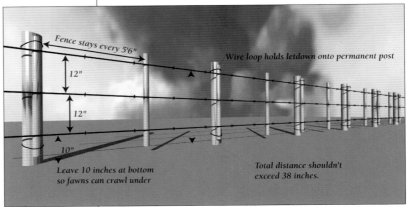

Letdown style fences allow easy passage in winter

erect a fence. Doubled fences are especially difficult for wildlife to pass. Fences in the interior of the property, such as around pastures or other divisions, should be low wooden types. Fences around yards, especially to keep dogs at home, can be impassable.

FENCES IN WINTER: With all fence types snow can accumulate to the point where a 38" fence becomes an 8" fence. Building high fences in anticipation of deep snow is harmful to the wildlife since most migrations occur when snow depth is minimal. If in doubt, build first for safe wildlife passage and then contain livestock or exclude wildlife in specific areas as needed.

Extricating wildlife from a Fence: The best thing is to call a state game official. Most wildlife that get caught are snared in barbed wire fences and the situation can be dangerous as the animal struggles to escape. If no help is available you can approach the animal cautiously and slowly so you won't frighten it and cut the fencing with heavy wire cutters. This usually requires cutting close to the animal's foot where the wire is twisted, so extreme caution should be taken not to get within reach of a thrashing foot. Often the animal will be exhausted and lying on the ground, and you can cover its head with a blanket to help keep it quiet. Remember that your approach may cause a renewed effort to escape, harming the animal or you as it thrashes.

DIFFERENT SPECIES' RESPONSES TO FENCES:

Each wildlife species treats a fence differently, so the landowner needs to be familiar with local wildlife before building a fence.
MOOSE usually step or jump over. They tend to wander more than follow a specific trail, so there needs to be a number of openings or sections that are passable.

DEER generally jump over fences, but will often go through as well, especially with a buckrail fence. Deer often cross a fence in the same place every day, so it is easy to select a specific stretch of fence to adapt for them.
PRONGHORN duck under or go through, and when spending time in one area will move predictably between grazing spots. Sometimes the fence on just one side of a property needs to be passable.
BISON go through fences at will and are also surprisingly agile jumpers. Setting heights and spacing won't necessarily insure that the bison will comply. Using the general guidelines for fence heights will at least give them the option of going over rather than through. Bison are wanderers but follow general seasonal routes from winter to summer range. They will also return to an inviting area of food, water and rubbing or wallowing spots.
ELK tend to go over a fence until the herd gains momentum, then the animals in back of the herd may charge through to keep up. Keeping fences low and visible and letting down large sections in critical areas, especially during fall migration, will help. During the rest of the year the number of elk involved is likely to be fewer and the pressure of migration will be absent.

Built up dirt mound

Very steep slope on fence side of mound

Animals running along fence will go up slope of mound and be diverted by perpendicular panel through opening in fence, jumping down steep part. They won't climb back out.

FENCE SPECIFICATIONS FOR EXCLUDING BIG GAME WILDLIFE

PURPOSE OF FENCE	FENCE SPECIFICATIONS*
Exclude **DEER, ELK** and **MOOSE** from garden, young trees, stored crops	*7' foot fence with 2 strands of smooth, 2 courses of woven wire*
Exclude **DEER** and **BLACK BEAR** from gardens, trees, beehives	*Electric fence with 5 to 6 strands, 3 or 4 that are hot*
Exclude **FOXES** and **COYOTES** from goats, poultry, or sheep	*Electric fence with 5 to 8 strands, 3 to 4 that are hot*
Exclude **DEER** from trees, gardens, young trees, or small fields	*Add 1 or 2 hot wires of electrical fence to existing fence*

*Fence specifications from Wyoming Game and Fish Department Habitat Extension Bulletin #53.

The "Moose-proof" Fence

Mike Kennedy worked for several years as the caretaker of a large vacation home near a golf course. The property had just been extensively landscaped with ornamental trees and shrubs when he moved in, and the first winter a small herd of moose arrived and began eating. Despite Mike's efforts to chase the moose off, by spring all the expensive vegetation was gone.

The next summer Mike was busy replanting and making plans to fend off the moose that coming winter. In the fall a landscape architect presented him with drawings for a guaranteed moose-proof fence. It was basically a buckrail fence with some modifications.

Mike built the buckrail part around all five acres and then added the proposed moose stopper, a series of sixteen-foot poles spaced every ten feet, leaning out over the fence and strung with electric fence wire. Moose nose height was determined to be six feet off the ground, and that's where the wire was placed. There was a strand of wire all the way around the perimeter with connectors down to a second wire. Mike bought the largest and most powerful transformer available and grounded it with a huge copper rod pounded into the ground. Even though the fence made the house look like a concentration camp, Mike enjoyed the effort of building it and

thought it would give him a few moose-free days to ski that winter.

The winter was fairly mild and the fence worked fine. The first moose to hit the wire turned around and went away and there were no more problems. In the spring Mike took the fence down and stored it away and confidently planted more small trees.

The next winter was more severe and the moose were more hungry. One day a big bull moose tried to ignore the first jolt of electricity and go through the fence, but he got entangled in the two buzzing wires and panicked. By the time he got free and stopped running he had pulled the entire five-acre electric fence down and dragged the wire a half-mile. The property was unprotected. Within a few days moose were coming in and the ornamental trees and shrubs started to disappear. Mike half-heartedly tried a few other measures and then gave up and went skiing. The moose had won.

What Mike remembers most about the whole episode is the reaction he got from a life-long rancher not long after he had finished the fence. Mike described his fence in detail while the rancher listened politely. When he finished, the rancher just smiled, shook his hand, and said, "Mike, good luck."

C.C.

The Moose and Fence

Jackie and Patrick Gilmore looked out their window one November morning to see a cow moose standing near the barbed wire fence that ran along the lane that led to their house. The fence surrounded an old hay field that was used for grazing cattle in the fall, and the fence was only periodically maintained. When Jackie looked with binoculars she could also see a large moose calf lying on the snow with one hind leg caught in the fence. The mother stood nearby.

Patrick got some heavy wire cutters and he and Jackie slowly drove their van toward the two moose. When they reached the calf, the cow moved off a short distance and watched. Patrick's driver's side door was only about eight feet away from the exhausted calf, which lay stretched out and unmoving on the snow. It's left hind foot had been caught between two strands of wire, and in its struggle to escape, the calf had twisted the wires tighter and tighter until they cut into the skin.

Jackie got out of the car with a blanket and stood next to the calf to throw the blanket over it's head to calm it in case it struggled. The calf didn't move while Patrick carefully snipped the wires, and it lay very still while he and Jackie got in the car and backed up the lane. They parked the car and waited while the cow moose returned to her calf, and the calf got up.

When the two moose walked away, Patrick and Jackie could see the calf putting its injured leg down, but the foot was turned under and caused it to limp badly. The wire had cut into the flesh all the way around the ankle.

They knew the moose had to go over another fence to get out of the pasture, so Patrick and Jackie drove ahead to watch. The cow jumped the next fence but the calf balked. The cow ran ahead and then returned, running up and down the fenceline. After several minutes the calf jumped and its hind feet hit the wire. Patrick's and Jackie's hearts sank, but the calf kicked free and managed to stay on his feet. Both moose trotted off, with the calf barely keeping up.

A few hours later Jackie saw them both in the sagebrush; the cow was feeding and the calf was lying down. Later that day they were gone, and although they never came back, Jackie assumed the rescue had been successful.

A Porcupine Story

Inger and Bob Koedt had a baby porcupine show up on their kitchen windowsill early one summer. The sill had a wide board attached as a bird feeder where the young porcupine sat. Inger felt sorry for it and fed it some bread. The porcupine stayed with them for fifteen years. It was a very sweet animal and would always greet them at the front door. One time they accidently left the door open while away and came home to find the porky sitting on their piano, waiting patiently for them to come home.

The porcupine brought others in the winter and at times there were as many as five big porcupines milling around on the front porch or on the shovelled walkway. Inger fed them all day-old bread. Visitors were often surprised to see the animals and many would stop in the trail when confronted. Most people changed their perception of porcupines through the encounters. Most of the animals were friendly but some of the newer ones were more aggressive, demanding to be fed, and they chewed up the Koedt's wooden screen door and wooden lawn furniture.

One winter night Bob and Inger had company for dinner and Bob served a bottle of expensive red wine. The wine was too cold, so Bob opened it and set it in the oven for a minute to warm up and breathe, but it got too warm so he set it outside in the snow to cool down again. When he went outside a few mintutes later to retrieve the wine he found an empty bottle and lots of porcupine tracks. The porcupine had tipped the bottle over, eaten the red snow and gotten tipsy. Bob found the winding trail where the porcupine had staggered off into the trees to sleep it off.

Inger quit feeding the porcupines but they continued to come around. Eventually, after fifteen years, the Koedt porcupine just stopped coming and Inger knew he was gone for good. She does not recommend feeding porcupines.

C.C.

CHAPTER NINE

Porcupines

Porcupines are chubby, slow moving rodents of the forest. Their back is high and arched, their legs are short, and their tail is broad. Much of their appearance is due to their quills and long guard hairs that spike out when the animals feel threatened. They waddle slowly on the ground, climb deliberately, and take

things at their own pace. Porcupines rely on their quills for protection but prefer to waddle quickly away rather than confront an enemy. If cornered or attacked they face away, with quills up and tail lashing back and forth. They cannot "throw" quills, but the barbed quills are released from the porcupine easily and imbed themselves deeply, especially if they come from a swipe of the powerful tail.

Porcupines are mostly nocturnal, solitary animals. They are active year-round and spend most of their time in and around trees. They eat chiefly tree bark and twigs in winter and a variety of other vegetation the rest of the year. They love salt and other mineral tastes, and are notorious for chewing up wooden axe and shovel handles where human sweat has left a salty residue. Plywood, with its resiny glue, is also popular. Porcupines breed in late fall and give birth in May or June.

PORCUPINE
RANGE

Erethizon dorsatum

PORCUPINES ON THE PROPERTY: The first indication a porcupine leaves is usually a patch of missing bark on a tree, often a pine, showing white where the bark is gone. These may seem to appear mysteriously at night, with no other signs. In winter the porcupine will leave small, oval-shaped tracks with claw marks half a paw length ahead of the prints. Porcupines can be particularly frustrating as they methodically strip the bark from one tree after another. The portion of tree above the stripped bark will die if the porcupine completely girdles the trunk. In a forested area they tend to switch from tree to tree often enough that the trees are not killed, but in a yard where there are just a few trees they can do considerable damage.

FEEDING PORCUPINES: Porcupines tame easily and become habituated to human food. They can become demanding until fed, and hang out waiting impatiently for food. While waiting they will gnaw on other things like doors, porches and wires. Feeding porcupines invariably causes problems, both for the animals and for you. They will also spend more time on the ground where dogs will encounter them. However, they can be fed briefly as a means of trapping and removing them.

PORCUPINES AND LANDSCAPING:

Porcupines will eat about anything growing, but they prefer to be up in a tree eating bark. They usually are a problem around houses only in winter, when trees are the only available vegetation. They can wander, following the salt and green shoots of growth along roadsides and may be found miles from forested areas.

DISCOURAGING PORCUPINES:

Fences help somewhat, whether smooth wooden fences or wire mesh, but porcupines are skilled climbers. An entire yard can be fenced or just individual trees enclosed. Sheet metal wrapped around the base of a tree will keep porcupines from climbing. Porcupines can be caught fairly easily with a garbage can by placing it over the animal and then sliding the lid under as you tip it up, or by herding the animal into a can lying on the ground. It can then be safely transported and released. The slow-moving porcupine can also be herded out of a yard using the spray from a garden hose. Once a porcupine is up in a tree there is little you can do except wait for it to climb down.

Porcupines are extremely sensitive to plant chemistry. They live in a world of the taste and smell of vegetation and the presence of salts. You can decoy porcupines away from specific areas or from plants by providing a salty piece of wood. Saline solution used for contact lenses is the proper saltiness and can be poured on a piece of wood to be used as bait. With this you can lure a porcupine away from landscaped trees or into a live trap.

Porcupines are attracted to the salty wood of axe handles and butterchurns

Porcupines become demanding if you start feeding them

CHAPTER TEN

Wolf

Coyotes, Foxes and Wolves

Wild members of the dog family vary greatly in their relationship to humans and in their presence around residential areas. The larger gray wolf is a rare and elusive animal and its appearance near residences would be unusual, while the abundant coyote can show up anywhere, even in the middle of a town.

Foxes are fairly common but are usually seen only around farms and ranches.

WOLVES: Wolves are carnivores, killing deer, elk, and moose and also smaller animals like rabbits, beavers, and birds. They may also prey on domestic livestock. A positive wolf sighting should not only be enjoyed and remembered, but should be reported to wildlife officials to help promote the wolf's return to a natural place in our world. The wolf was practically exterminated from the West by the 1940s and is only now making a slow and sporadic return. Old grudges and confusion with coyotes prevents the wolves from regaining much of a foothold.

COYOTES: Widespread and common, coyotes seem to thrive on adversity. They are smart and adaptable, and even though they are hunted for their fur and killed as a livestock predator, they continue to expand their range. Increasing development into coyote habitat brings more contact with these animals.

COYOTE
RANGE

Canis latrans

Coyotes will eat almost anything. They catch mice and ground squirrels, birds and insects, and they eat carrion. They also eat some plants. They prey on weak and young deer, elk, and livestock, and they feed on dead wildlife, sheep, and cattle. They have been known to snatch domestic pets from yards in times of hunger, and they will lure domestic dogs away from safety by taunting them, and then kill them.

Coyotes are associated with the wide-open spaces of the west, and their howls, yips, and barks bring a thrill in more suburban areas. Coyotes readily become accustomed to humans, especially if there is food involved, so they should not be fed or baited. They can become bold and aggressive if cut off from an habitual food source.

FOXES: Less visible and not as numerous as coyotes, foxes don't form into packs like wolves or gather in numbers like coyotes. They eat primarily mice and other rodents, and rabbits. Foxes are fairly quiet, shy residents. They may den close to or under ranch buildings

Fox in the barnyard

or in a burrow near homes in rural settings. Foxes are more prone to rabies and distemper than coyotes or wolves, so avoid any fox that appears tame or acts strangely.

ENCOURAGING COYOTES OR FOXES: About the best you can do is leave them alone. You can make sure there is no predator eradication program on your property and find out what is being done on neighboring land. Ranchers and farmers may be using one of several means of controlling coyote numbers and you should be aware of the devices used. *(See Wildlife Population Control, p. 44)* Attracting deer, elk, or moose to your property in the winter through native landscaping may bring coyotes to feed on the inevitable winter-killed ungulates.

RED FOX
RANGE
Vulpes vulpes

Foxes may be encouraged somewhat by providing log and brush piles or leaving old buildings like sheds or barns for den sites. Coyotes and foxes both feed extensively on rodents, especially voles and ground squirrels, so a meadow or fallow field full of mice may be an attraction.

If you think you have a coyote or fox den on your property you can observe it from a distance with binoculars to make sure—and then leave that area alone. Coyotes are especially sensitive to disturbances near their dens and will move pups to a new den.

Coyotes and foxes generally don't mix well with domestic dogs. Most large breeds will keep their wild cousins at a distance, but there are many cases where dogs and coyotes or dogs and foxes have played and run together.

tree-climbing coyote

Thanksgiving, and we were still hiking. Snow two weeks old dusted the upper slopes of Monument Ridge and retreated into hardened lumps under the sagebrush. Dove-gray clouds, thin enough to let the sunlight through, spread across the sky. The aspens that had set the hills ablaze a few weeks earlier stood bare. We hiked a spur ridge toward the top, dry grass and flower stalks crunching underfoot. We sat on a log for lunch, making little conversation, grateful for another day of bare ground on which to walk.

Across a draw and through the aspens, we caught a glimpse of movement—a coyote trotting down the hillside directly toward us. He slinked along with head and tail down, not pausing to sniff at rodent holes: had he smelled our sandwiches instead? But the coyote ignored us, or hadn't caught our scent. From the crest of the ridge beyond the draw, two mule deer appeared, also at a trot. They looked as if they were following the coyote. They picked up speed and purposefully marched side by side through the aspens.

"Those deer must see the coyote," I whispered. Their ears stood erect and their gaze never wavered. Soon it became clear that they not only saw him, they were after him. They closed in while the coyote trotted faster and held his ears low. All three continued to stride toward Don and me, the coyote not more than two hundred feet away.

Suddenly he sprang straight up and into an aspen tree. "Did you see that," Don hissed, "a tree-climbing coyote!" The coyote teetered on a small angled branch that didn't look strong enough to hold him. The does slowed, ears erect, their feet stamping. "They want to kick his butt," Don whispered. The coyote didn't move.

The wind came up, giving us away. The deer abruptly wheeled and bounded back up the draw. The coyote waited, either wondering or realizing what had scared them off, then jumped out of the aspen tree and loped away.

By Susan L. Marsh

Red Fox

Wildlife Population Control

In the absence of human interference, a healthy wildlife population is regulated naturally through predation, disease, limited food and habitat, and a compensating change in birth rates. Most wild species go through cycles of high and low numbers over the years. When certain species deemed undesirable by humans,

such as starlings or rodents, reach high populations they are controlled by other means. Unfortunately, unless there is some drastic habitat change that makes an area unfit for one of these unwanted species, the only effective way to control numbers is to kill all the targeted animals in a large area. Populations of some species, like coyotes, are kept constantly in check by this method.

Government-run control programs have developed a variety of devices for controlling, or killing wildlife that prey on livestock or damages crops. As residential development continues to consume large tracts of agricultural land and push into the edges of forest and rangeland, the chances of homeowners being affected by some of these control methods increases.

The following are some of the primary methods of control. While none of these methods is recommended, they are in use and you should be aware of them. Any suspected control device you find should be left alone and a wildlife official contacted. Most pets are susceptible to these devices and should be restrained on your property if a control program is taking place on neighboring land.

COYOTE GETTER OR CYANIDE GUN: This is a small, thumb-sized cylinder stuck into the ground and charged with firearm ammunition or a powerful spring. Rather than firing a bullet, the coyote getter shoots a fatal dose of sodium cyanide into the coyote's open mouth. The above-ground portion of this device is the trigger and is covered with a foul-smelling baited piece of fur or cloth resembling a meat scrap. It is designed to explode when the top of the cylinder is grabbed in the coyote's mouth and pulled up. Coyote getters are efficient and deadly to coyotes, but are also found by foxes, dogs, raccoons, skunks, bears, and other non-targeted predators and scavengers. Coyote getters are often found around the perimeters of ranchland and along stream bottoms and benches where coyotes live or travel. They are not affected by weather and may sit idle for a long time, remaining set and armed. The main danger to humans is injury from the explosive shell. Although coyote getters should be marked with warning signs nearby, often they are not.

STEEL TRAPS: The traditional steel trap is still a widely used method of control. In addition to predator control they are also used to trap fur-bearing animals like muskrats and beaver. Laws require the regular checking of traps to avoid suffering by the trapped animals, but traps are occasionally neglected, abandoned, or lost. The concern is for children, domestic pets, and non-target wildlife. Traps found near dwellings or in recreational use areas can be safely released with a stick and game officers notified. It is against the law to spring a legally placed trap, so you should investigate the source of any traps before attempting to disarm them.

POISON: There is a variety of poison used for wildlife control, and although most of it targets specific animals, there is always a chance of pets, humans, and non-target wildlife being accidentally poisoned. Poisons commmonly used include general toxicants like strychnine, compound 1080, and zinc phosphide, plus more specific ones like DRC-1339 for starlings and anticoagulants like Warfarin for rodents.

Gophers and other rodents are controlled by placing poison grain near their burrows or underground in their tunnels, and for the most part the bait is selective when used correctly. However, poisoned animals can be eaten by non-target predators and scavengers or pets and they, in turn, die from secondary poisoning.

If you find anything you think is a poison, or if you suspect a wild animal or your pet has eaten poison, call a game official to investigate. Indiscriminate poisoning of animals is unlawful.

above: Coyote hung on fence after being killed

below: Coyote dead after being caught in steel trap

CHAPTER TWELVE

Prairie Falcon

Birds

To a homeowner, the mention of birds usually brings to mind the bird-feeder variety: colorful, seed-eating songbirds that have no impact other than their bright plumage and welcome vocalization. But there is a great variety of birds, depending on the habitat and season, and some of them may go unnoticed until

you actively look for them.

—There are YEAR-ROUND RESIDENTS like chickadees that nest, raise their young and remain through the winter in one area. They may move from higher elevations to lower or may move to a new habitat for the winter.

—There are SEASONAL RESIDENTS like the mountain bluebird that arrive in the spring to nest and then depart with their young in the fall.

—There are also WINTER RESIDENTS like waxwings that come from colder climates and remain only through the worst of winter.

—There are MIGRANTS, birds passing through on their way to nesting or wintering grounds. Waterfowl species are good examples.

—There are ACCIDENTALS like snowy owls that appear only under certain conditions, such as cold and famine in their native arctic.

—And there are RECLUSIVE birds like the nocturnal owls and nighthawks.

In general, bird life has very little effect on a home, dwelling or property, but the condition of these areas can greatly affect life for the birds.

BENEFITS OF HAVING BIRDS: Insect-eating birds can have a significant impact on the numbers of mosquitos, moths, and flies. Providing nesting and shelter for certain bird species can preclude having to use insecticides. A few of the more effective insect eaters in the intermountain area are swallows and bluebirds.

Raptors, such as hawks and owls, will keep rodent numbers in check. The great-horned owl is one of the few predators that regularly kill skunks. Scavengers like the raven and magpie help keep the landscape clean of animals that die.

The calls of songbirds in the morning and evening add much to the atmosphere of a home and yard. Like many of the more delicate expressions of nature, birdsongs are often not noticed until they are gone.

PROBLEMS ASSOCIATED WITH BIRDS: Bird troubles are usually minor and include nuisances such as droppings or unwanted nests on the house, especially the mud bowls built by cliff swallows under the eaves. Large colonies of cliff swallows on homes can occasionally cause an infestation of mites that can enter a living space. Swallows can be discouraged by hanging chimes,

Mountain Bluebird

ribbons or netting under the eaves, but the most effective means is to prevent the building of mud nests in the first place.

A water hose with a spray nozzle used daily as the swallows first arrive is a safe and effective means of discouraging them, before they build a nest. Usually two or three days of disturbance will move them to another location. Once the nest is nearly completed you risk killing eggs or young. Swallows, along with most other birds, are protected by the U.S. Migratory Bird Act of 1918. A permit from the U.S. Fish and Wildlife Service is also required to remove any bird nests, including nests under construction, completed nests, or ones abandoned after the season.

Woodpeckers can damage the wood and plaster siding on a house as they look for insects or try to build nesting cavities. Flickers, one type of woodpecker, are notoriously loud and persistent at pecking holes in wood siding. Flickers can be discouraged from a new hole by applying a coating of non-toxic, sticky gel. Greenhouses sell this material to prevent climbing insects from reaching plants.

Woodpeckers can sometimes be distracted by providing a flat board for them to use. This "drumming" on a hollow sounding object is part of their territorial and mating behavior. In some locations woodpeckers drum on metal power poles, garbage can lids, or old pipes. Providing suet at a feeding site will help localize their activity.

Another concern with birds around homes is the destruction of gardens and flowering plants. Since these problems are seasonal it is easier to use temporary netting or scare tactics to move the birds. Unless birds get accustomed to a particular noise or visual disturbance they will move in

Northern flickers (shown at left) can be discouraged from a new hole by applying a coating of non-toxic, sticky gel. Greenhouses sell this material to prevent climbing insects from reaching plants. (See note on page 26)

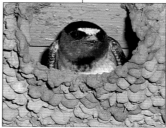

Swallows are protected by law—it's illegal to remove a nest.

Bohemian waxwings and other birds are attracted to wild fruit.

search of better feeding areas. There are a number of commercially available devices and repellents available for birds. Contact a local Game and Fish office for information. In extreme cases specific poisons are available for eliminating small flocks of crop-damaging birds such as starlings. However, these chemical methods invariably go beyond their intended scope and affect other species as well, so they are not recommended.

ATTRACTING BIRDS: There is plenty of literature available on building bird feeders and birdhouses. Libraries and bookstores are two good sources. In general you can provide commercially available birdseed for songbirds and suet for birds like jays and woodpeckers. Different seeds attract different birds, so determine which bird species you want to attract, or else provide several feeders with a variety of seeds. Nesting boxes for bluebirds, wrens, chickadees, or swallows are easy to build and once used will become traditional nesting sites.

You can plant seed-producing vegetation and fruit, and you can grow plants that provide shelter and nesting cover. The best long-term program to attract and keep birds is to provide them with a good variety of native plants that offer both food and cover. Planting in rows that act as a windbreak with adjacent shrubs to provide food varies the vegetation and offers a better chance for use. (*See Landscaping, p. 86*)

A good example of a cross-section of a planting for birds in this region is described below:
-*Pine, fir and blue spruce for high cover;*
-*Mountain ash, chokecherry, golden currant and serviceberry for seed and fruit eaters;*
-*Bitterbrush and rabbitbrush for seed eaters;*
-*Snowbrush and juniper for ground cover;*
-*A variety of native grasses and flowers such as wheatgrass, fescue, buckwheat and various sunflowers.*

If there is room on your property for perching and nesting sites such as dead or fallen trees and snags, these may provide for additional bird species. (*See Landscaping, p. 86*)

WINDOWS: Windows often appear to birds as reflections of the surrounding landscape. When frightened, birds can strike the window with enough speed either to break their necks or cause a severe concussion. Windows on the corner of a house provide birds with a clear view but an invisible, impenetrable barrier.

You can do a number of things to reduce the injuries from impact with glass. Move your bird feeders away from windows or place them near smaller windows with more noticeable edges, mark windows with cut-outs of birds in flight, or hang chimes or other decoration in front of the windows. Fiberglass mosquito netting over a large window will break the reflection and is no more obtrusive than a screen. A house with extensive glass is bound to kill a number of birds every year. Bird feeders are the most common culprit, especially in wooded areas where raptor species like sharp-shinned and Cooper's hawks prey on small birds. The panic induced by an attacking hawk can drive anything, including the hawk, into a window. (*See Uncle Bert Raynes' Advice, p. 18*)

WATERFOWL: Waterfowl can be considered either nesting residents on a pond or stream on your property, or visitors such as migrating swans, geese or ducks. For migratory species the best thing you can do is to provide adequate water levels with protected areas like islands, and plant lots of natural food like sedges and grasses. Leave as much unmowed vegetation as you can, especially close to the water. If they like the area and are not disturbed, waterfowl will nest and continue to return each year. Platforms for geese and nesting boxes for wood ducks, goldeneyes, and mergansers will encourage them to stay. Remember that fences crossing waterways are of particular danger to diving ducks and large waterfowl such as swans.

In the winter, flocks of geese and ducks may gather on municipal

American Wigeon

Mallard

Ring-necked Duck

Common Merganser

Canada Goose

ponds and golf courses or in vacant hayfields and pastures. Again, planting natural vegetation for food will attract and keep them. Artificial feeding of waterfowl with corn or other seeds tends to tame them and make them easier prey for domestic dogs and cats as well as building an artificially large population in a place that can't support them. Then, if you stop feeding them, many will die. Large numbers of geese can cause damage to streamsides, meadows, and crops.

HUMMINGBIRDS: Summer residents in the intermountain west, hummingbirds winter in the southern United States and Mexico. There are many different species but all rely on plant nectar to fuel their flight. They also eat numerous small insects for protein. Hummingbirds are easily attracted to a feeder that dispenses sugar water and will return every year to the same feeder. The benefits of feeding hummingbirds is doubtful, especially when using refined white sugar as the food source. Their extremely high metabolism burns up calories so fast that they must also feed on natural nectar and catch insects. More problems occur from improper ratios of sugar to water (one part sugar to four parts water is correct; never use honey) and from flying into windows adjacent to feeders.

If more than one feeder is used they must be placed far apart to prevent territorial fighting. A good alternative to feeders is to plant attractive wildflowers or

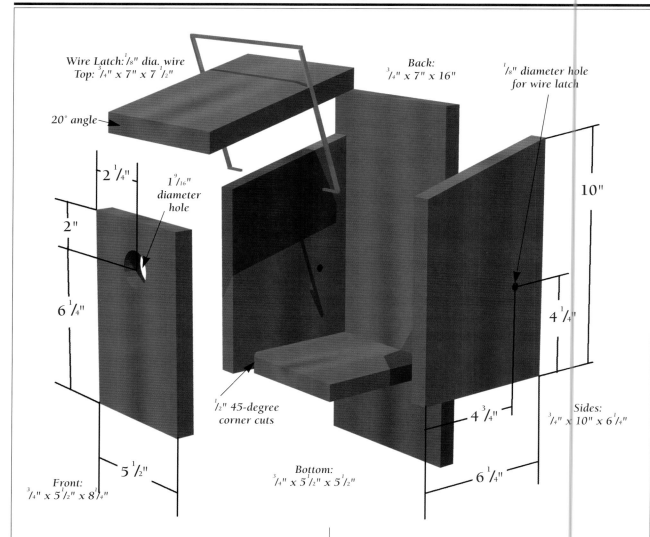

Wire Latch: $^1/_8$" dia. wire
Top: $^3/_4$" x 7" x 7 $^1/_2$"

20° angle

2 $^1/_4$"

1 $^9/_{16}$" diameter hole

2"

6 $^1/_4$"

5 $^1/_2$"

Front:
$^3/_4$" x 5 $^1/_2$" x 8 $^1/_4$"

$^1/_2$" 45-degree corner cuts

Bottom:
$^3/_4$" x 5 $^1/_2$" x 5 $^1/_2$"

Back:
$^3/_4$" x 7" x 16"

$^1/_8$" diameter hole for wire latch

10"

4 $^1/_4$"

4 $^3/_4$"

6 $^1/_4$"

Sides:
$^3/_4$" x 10" x 6 $^1/_4$"

DO'S AND DON'TS OF BUILDING A BLUEBIRD HOUSE

DO:

1. Place the box 3 $^1/^2$ to 4 $^1/^2$ feet above ground level.
2. Whenever possible, face box towards a small tree or shrub. If a fence post is used, face box lengthwise of the fence when possible. If a telephone or power pole is used, face box lengthwise of the lines. This establishes perch sites for the male when female is brooding. Ideal distance from the box to perch is five to one hundred feet. Face box away from prevailing winds.
3. Use fences near or above cliffs and clay banks found along streams and rivers. These areas may have natural nesting bluebirds that will respond quickly to boxes.
4. Place boxes in pasture or short grass areas. Remember, bluebirds forage on the ground to secure food for their young.
5. If you use a single tree, be sure it's far enough from dense trees to avoid squirrel depredation.
6. Clean boxes out after each fledge if

possible, or at least each fall to avoid mites and fly larvae attacking young birds. Drill 1/4" holes in the bottom of the box for ventilation or drainage.

DON'T:

1. Avoid placing boxes near thickets of thorn apple, chokecherry or wild roses or the juniper clumps found in dryer areas, as this is house wren habitat and they destroy bluebird nests.
2. Don't put boxes near summer fallow or wheat crop areas as there is no feed available and there is a danger from spray.
3. Avoid dense posts with braces running to the ground as weasels and chipmunks can readily run up to the box.
4. Avoid heavy timbered areas and areas of heavy ground cover.
5. Avoid areas close to stagnant ponds and swampy areas because tree swallows will claim the houses.
6. Keep boxes 1/4 mile from feedlots and homes because of cats and sparrows.

Adapted from Mountain Bluebird Trails, by Art Aylesworth and Deni Hershberger

non-native flowering plants like allysum, scarlet lobelia, honeysuckle, or delphinium. Hummingbird feeders also attract bees and wasps. Bee guards are available for many feeders. Insects sprays should not be used.

Red-Tailed Hawk

RAPTORS: Raptors are birds of prey and include hawks, owls, and eagles. They have been given a bad reputation, and have been shot and poisoned as killers of domestic pets, fowl, and livestock. They actually prey mostly on rodents, and a few resident raptors will help keep mouse and ground squirrel populations in check. The preferred action is not to disturb them, especially around their nests. Leaving snags and hollow trees also helps. In one instance a homeowner in a treeless, open development placed a long log upright in the ground, sticking up about twenty feet, and nailed on several "branches" to create a dead snag. Within a day a hawk found the artificial tree and began using it regularly as a hunting perch for the numerous ground squirrels in the homeowner's yard. You do not need to poison or trap rodents if there is a raptor active in your area.

CROWS, JAYS, AND RAVENS: The crow family is an interesting group of birds that often take up residence near homes. It includes crows, ravens, magpies, jays and the Clark's nutcracker. All of these birds are vocal, intelligent, and adaptable. Crows and ravens are considered the most intelligent of all birds. They are often treated as pests, probably because of their loud and aggressive nature, but they are beneficial as they eat a variety of insects, rodents, and carrion. Jays or magpies can dominate a bird feeder and chase off songbirds, so a second feeder with suet can be used to separate the bird species. For another perspective on this intelligent bird family read *Ravens in Winter* by Bernd Heinrich.

Raven

Hawk Visitor

Red-Tailed
Hawk

It was the spring of 1994 and, as usual, there were many birds migrating through Jackson Hole. We had hundreds of birds stop at our feeder on their journeys elsewhere. We hung large, colorful wind socks outside each picture window to break up the reflection of the surrounding forest in the glass. Still, on several occasions, a small bird would crash into one of our windows. When this happened, I would run outside and pick up the bird, hold it in my hands and send it love. It would be stunned from the impact and often unconscious. However, after a few minutes of holding it and stroking its back, it would usually revive and fly off.

Very early one morning while I was still asleep, my husband, George, yelled up to me from downstairs. "Barbara, wake up!" I turned over trying to ignore him, but I heard his call again. "Quick! Come down right away! Please hurry! There is a bird outside on the deck that has run into the window." I rolled out of bed and started to wake. "Really hurry! It's different from all the others," he called frantically.

By now I was fully awake. I grabbed my robe from the back of the bathroom door and threw it on, and raced down the stairs. George met me at the bottom . "This bird is unlike any we've seen," he said as his eyes grew larger and larger. "This bird is big."

I opened the glass door and stepped barefooted onto the redwood deck. Lying on the deck below the picture window was a large bird. A very large bird. "This isn't just a big bird," I told him. "This is a hawk."

I looked at the beautiful, gray hawk with red and white markings on his breast and belly. His black talons were aimed straight to the sky, as he lay unconscious on his back. His head was lying to one side, displaying a beautiful, hooked bill with a little black tip. A thought flashed through my mind as to whether I should be picking up a hawk who uses his bill and talons for tearing apart flesh. I quickly dismissed the thought.

I gathered the hawk up in my hands, holding him underneath his back and lifting him to my chest. His yellow legs were dangling from his body. George pulled up a wooden deck chair for me and I sat down. The hawk's heart was pressed to mine and I could feel it beating incredibly fast. Beat, beat, beat, beat, beat against my heart. I used my right hand to hold him next to me while I gently stroked him with my left, from his crown all the way down his back. Stroke, stroke, stroke. All during this time, I was sending him love. "You will be fine," I said reassuringly. "You will be just fine and will be flying soon."

For thirty minutes I sat in the chair and stroked the hawk's back while George stood and watched intently. Suddenly George's expression changed.

"He's opening his eyes, Barbara," he whispered with amazement. "He's opening his eyes and looking at us. But wait! There is something wrong with his right eye! He is trying to see, but he can't! The impact against the window must have blinded him."

I looked down but it was hard to see what was happening from my vantage point. So I twisted my neck to get a better view. "Why, there's a feather jammed in his eye!" I said with astonishment.

I reached down with my left hand and took hold of the small, downy, gray feather. I pulled it out of the hawk's eye and placed it on the post of the deck railing. There was blood on the end that had been imbedded in his eye.

"He can see!" George exclaimed.

I continued my stroking motion down the crown and back of the hawk. Suddenly I felt pressure against my right hand with which I had been holding him to my chest. The hawk was pushing his wings against me. I placed both my hands on his body and lifted him high into the air, releasing him to the heavens. He flew. He made a complete circle in the air above us and then disappeared.

I was never so humbled in my life. It was such an honor to have held a wild bird—a hawk—in my arms. To feel his heart against mine had been incredible. I walked around during the rest of the day, surrounded by a feeling of true grace. When I went to bed that night, I thanked the universe for the experience of magic—magic that I had known as a child.

The next morning as I awoke and put on my robe, I remembered the wondrous experience of the day before. I descended the stairs, slowly this time, and looked out onto the deck where I had held the hawk. There on the deck railing where I had placed the feather from his eye, sat the hawk. Our eyes met through the glass of the living room window and locked. After a couple of minutes he turned his head and flew off, making the same circle in the air before he disappeared.

By Barbara Erbe

Spotted Skunk

Skunks

Except for their smell, skunks are pretty unobtrusive neighbors. They are largely nocturnal, coming out of burrows and from beneath buildings to feed on mice, insects, grubs, and bird's eggs as well as getting into garbage, compost, and pet and livestock food. During the winter skunks are inactive, living mostly on stored

body fat and remaining in their dens. They breed in late winter, and the young are born in mid-spring. They live mostly in lower elevations, in woodlands and around farms and suburbs. Skunks like to den under older buildings, porches, and sheds. Avoid any skunk that appears unafraid as it may have rabies.

SKUNK SMELL: Skunks have a scent gland at the base of the tail and can spray an oily musk ten to fifteen feet. The musk causes temporary loss of vision and fierce pain if it hits the eyes, protecting the skunk from predators. Skunks spray when frightened or attacked, and raise their tail straight in the air to expose the scent gland.

Humans are usually sprayed only when they surprise a skunk in the garbage or on the porch. A skunk hit by a car will cause the car to smell for days, as well as stinking up the occupants and the general area.

Dogs are often sprayed as they attack a slow-moving

SPOTTED SKUNK
RANGE

Spilogale gracilis

skunk, and the dog will usually charge back into the house, bringing the odor with them. As they do with porcupines, some dogs persist in chasing skunks and get sprayed again and again. Skunk smell on pets can be washed out with mild soap followed with tomato juice or vinegar or with commercially available treatments. Veterinarians and pet stores usually carry these treatments. Ammonia, bleach, vinegar, or tomato juice will neutralize most odor on clothing or other objects.

LIVING WITH SKUNKS: Skunks are relatively harmless. Unless they are denning under your house you may not even know they are present except for an occasional whiff of skunk smell. They feed primarily on insects and mice if left to a natural diet. If no dogs are present and you learn where the skunks are living you can establish a live-and-let-live policy. Keep your garbage out of reach, use a covered or fenced composter and keep pet food locked away. Gardens can be protected by digging a fence down eighteen to twenty inches into the soil.

DISCOURAGING SKUNKS: It is the threat of a good spraying that makes skunks such unwelcome neighbors. One dose of skunk smell can linger for weeks. If there are skunks under your house or on the property you can live-trap them and remove them to a remote spot. Canned cat food or tuna makes a good bait. Check first with state game officials before relocating any trapped animal, as it is illegal to release some species in a new place. Skunks will normally not spray in a live trap if they are approached slowly and the cage is quietly covered. You can also tape cardboard over the trap before setting it.

Mothballs thrown under a building will reportedly move the skunks out temporarily while the foundation is sealed up. Check the warnings on the mothball container to be sure the type of mothball being used doesn't release toxic fumes.

STRIPED SKUNK
RANGE

Mephitis mephitis

Ammonia placed in a jar with a sponge wick also works. Not even skunks like these smells.

If you are patient you can watch to see where and when the skunks leave your dwelling and then seal the opening when they leave. Sprinkle fine dirt or flour in front of the opening to check for tracks. Make sure that there are no young skunks remaining behind. This often requires waiting until mid or late summer when the young will be actively leaving the den. If you are sure of the entrance hole you can attach a simple hinged board over the hole so the animals can get out but not back in. Great-horned owls are one of the skunk's few natural predators. These owls live in the woods and hunt in clearings, meadows, and yards. They prefer to nest in large hollow trees or in an open cavity of a snag. Encouraging predators like the great horned owl, through habitat preservation and a policy of not using rodent poisons, is the best long-term method of controlling unwelcome skunks.

Young Striped Skunks

Evie's Skunk

When Evie Lewis moved into her home she found she had inherited a skunk problem. The small guest house had no foundation and over the years skunks had found their way underneath and denned there. The former owner had waged a war, trapping and shooting skunks each summer.

Evie's first problem was a lack of information on skunks. She knew she had to get rid of them, but she wasn't sure where to start. Pest control services charged a lot of money and rental traps were often not available when needed. After asking around she finally decided the best approach was to live-trap the animals one by one and then humane-ly drown them in a garbage can full of water by dropping in the entire trap. She bought her own live trap and a new garbage can big enough to hold the trap. Her husband put off setting the trap, so one night Evie set it herself next to the guest house. This was her first trapping experience.

The next morning there was a young skunk in the trap. The trap was confining enough that the skunk couldn't spray, and there was no smell. Evie carried the trap over and set it in the can, stuck the end of the garden hose in, and turned it on. She realized she couldn't watch, and went in to the house to wait.

After a few minutes she looked out and saw water overflowing from the garbage can and knew the skunk must be drowned. She went out to remove the trap and dispose of the body, but just as she opened the door she saw the skunk, soaking wet and bedraggled and mad, running right at her. It had somehow escaped from the trap. Just as she slammed the door the skunk sprayed at her, cover-ing the front steps and porch with musk.

Evie decided she would relocate skunks after that, and successfully trapped and moved five skunks. Then she and her husband dug an eigh-teen-inch-deep trench all around the guest house and set chicken wire in it extending up onto the house. They waited until night and the last skunk was gone before they sealed up the final hole, and they never had another skunk after that.

C.C.

Skunk Release

The National Park Service has a reputation for helping their neighbors and in-holders and will go to great lengths to foster good relationships.

An in-holder adjacent to one of our nation's western parks was having a lot of trouble with skunks under the porch of his residence, store, restaurant and bar. The skunk was getting into garbage cans at night and spraying everything and everybody that passed by. The odor permeated the entire area and customers were complaining and were not too pleased with the prospect of walking headlong into one of the area's smelliest nocturnal inhabitants.

The park developed a new skunk trap designed to keep out the light and with so tight a fit that a skunk could not lift its tail to spray once the door closed. Hearing of the park's success in live-trapping skunks, a call was made by the in-holder requesting help. The park eagerly sent the area ranger with the baited trap and it was left in the skunk's path.

The very next morning, the park received a call from the jubilant in-holder informing them of the success of the operation. The trap door was closed and there was movement inside.

The ranger carefully carried the trap to the patrol vehicle and transported it to an overlook several miles from any development before releas-ing it. A ranger in a patrol car always gathers crowds and this was no exception. The crowd was advised to stand back for the release and the ranger lifted the door to the trap. The in-holder's beautiful orange tabby, flew from the opening and with a yowl, disappeared into the woods.

After checking the next morning and finding the tabby back home on the front porch of the store, the ranger took all the credit for the brilliant handling of the "skunk situation." As the cat had returned and the skunk didn't, there didn't seem to be any reason to mention that the park seemed to have also developed a great live-trap for pet cats.

S.M.

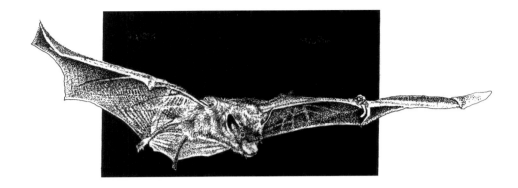

CHAPTER FOURTEEN

Bats

Bats are so surrounded by frightening myths and evil folklore that it is difficult for many people to think of them as wildlife. But they are just small, nocturnal mammals that are able to fly. Their rate of carrying rabies is less than that of most pets, and when they are healthy and undisturbed we hardly know they

are there. Bats are not blind, as the old saying goes, but rely more on their unusul hearing and echolocation to navigate in the dim light. Bats are seen at twilight and early dawn and at night flitting around outdoor lights where flying insects gather. They roost during the day in dark spaces and also have night roosts for the hours when insect activity slows down. Caves, attics, and other hollows are preferred roosts. Many bat species hibernate through the winter while others migrate to warmer regions.

Bats in this region are insect eaters, and it is estimated that one bat eats anywhere from three thousand to seven thousand insects a night. Different bat species specialize in catching moths, beetles, or other insect species. They are shy, harmless animals saddled with an undeserved bad reputation.

BATS ON THE PROPERTY: You may not know there are bats around unless they enter the home or attic and become a nuisance. Because bats are nocturnal their appearance during the day is unusual and causes concern. A bat that flies in through an open door at night or roosts at dawn in a darkened room can cause a difficult time for a homeowner. Young bats may become confused as they disperse from the main roosts, trying to sleep in small cracks and under things, and end up on your lawn or drive-way in daylight. Any bat found on the ground, especially one unable to fly, should be treated with caution. Leather gloves should be worn if handling a bat, and any bat bite needs to be treated and the bat examined by a veterinarian for disease.

Bats are able to crawl though incredibly narrow cracks to find a safe, dark roost. A large number of bats can produce annoying noises as they scratch around and squeak, and their feces and urine can be unpleasant close to a living space. Unfortunately, there is no good way to evict bats; repellents, lights, chemicals, and ventilation are only moderately successful.

The only sure way is to let the animals leave on their own and then block their re-entry points. Once they're out, the attic must be sealed with screen over the ventilation holes and every crack down to a quarter inch sealed with caulk or metal flashing. Cracks can be sealed in the evening when careful observation may reveal the point of their entry and exit. This should not be done in June and July when the young, flightless bats are likely to be inside.

Otherwise they can be easily discouraged by hanging half-inch nylon bird netting over the area of the bats' entry holes. The netting should extend a foot or so on all sides of the entry hole and should hang freely several inches from the building wall. The bats will be able to crawl out and under the netting to leave but unable to fly back up under it, thus creating a one-way bat door. Most bats in the United States leave their roost sites in the fall, allowing you all winter to seal the buildings.

Bats are generally misunderstood and unappreciated. While large government grants go toward saving larger and more dramatic animal species, very little money is designated for bats. By providing a safe and permanent roosting site you can help offset this imbalance and help keep these animals from extinction. It's an unglamorous but critical role.

Bats are particular about the structure and location of the house. They need certain sizes and roost temperatures, so you may have to move the house a few times to find a good location.

BAT SPECIES COMMON IN THE ROCKY MOUNTAINS

Little Brown Bat
Abundant, often roosts in buildings. Feeds on aquatic insects.

Big Brown Bat
Common, often roosts in buildings. Feeds on wide variety of flying insects, specializing in flying beetles.

Silver Haired Bat
Common, roosts in trees, occasionally in buildings. Feeds on a wide variety of flying insects.

Hoary Bat
Occasional, roosts in foliage of trees. Feeds on moths.

Long Eared Bat
Rare, roosts in caves, mines, buildings. Probably feeds on beetles.

Long-legged Bat
Common, roosts in buildings, trees, and rocks. Feeds on moths.

Western Small-footed Bat
A colony rooster. This bat eats moths and beetles.

Western Big-eared Bat
Rare. Eats moths and prefers caves or mines for roosting. Sensitive to roost disturbance.

NOTES ON BAT HOUSE PLACEMENT*

TEMPERATURE
Bats prefer warm day roosts, in the 80 to 90 degree F range.
■ Build the house carefully with tight fitting joints. Reduce drafts by sealing joints and gaps with silicone caulk.
■ Paint or stain very dark, even black, or cover with tar paper. Apply three coats to inhibit humidity changes inside. Let the paint or stain dry and sit for several weeks before use.
■ Place to receive more than 4 hours of direct sunlight daily, 8 to 12 hours seems to be preferred. Early morning sun is desirable. Most occupancy failures result from too little exposure to sun.

HEIGHT
Bats prefer the highest available sites.
■ Research has documented that houses more than 20 feet off the ground have a 70% occupancy rate. Houses 11 to 15 feet off the ground are occupied about half the time and the rate drops to 40% when houses are lower than 10 feet.

LOCATION
Bats prefer day roosts that are near feeding areas.
■ Houses located within a quarter of a mile of a stream or river had a 78% occupancy rate. Running water seemed to be preferred over ponds or lakes. Larger ponds (over three acres) are preferred to smaller.
■ Receiving direct sunlight seems to be more important than whether the house is mounted on a pole, tree or building. However, houses mounted on trees are rarely if ever occupied. Bats prefer locations at least 20 feet away from flight obstacles.

*by Tom Haraden, South District Naturalist, Grand Teton National Park. Ref: The Bat House Builder's Handbook by Merlin D. Tuttle and Donna Hensley, available from Bat Conservation International, PO Box 162603, Austin TX 78716

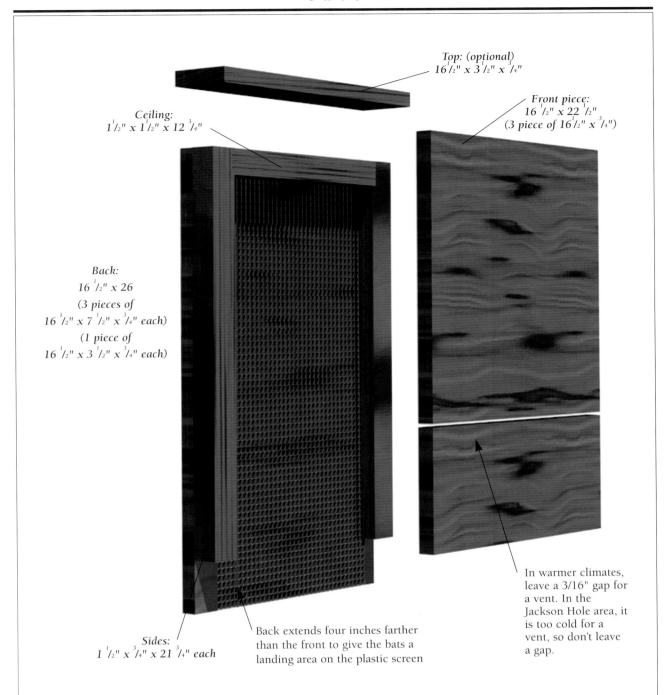

Top: (optional)
$16\frac{1}{2}$" x $3\frac{1}{2}$" x $\frac{3}{4}$"

Front piece:
$16\frac{1}{2}$" x $22\frac{1}{2}$"
(3 piece of $16\frac{1}{2}$" x $\frac{3}{4}$")

Ceiling:
$1\frac{1}{2}$" x $1\frac{1}{2}$" x $12\frac{3}{4}$"

Back:
$16\frac{1}{2}$" x 26
(3 pieces of
$16\frac{1}{2}$" x $7\frac{1}{2}$" x $\frac{3}{4}$" each)
(1 piece of
$16\frac{1}{2}$" x $3\frac{1}{2}$" x $\frac{3}{4}$" each)

In warmer climates, leave a 3/16" gap for a vent. In the Jackson Hole area, it is too cold for a vent, so don't leave a gap.

Back extends four inches farther than the front to give the bats a landing area on the plastic screen

Sides:
$1\frac{1}{2}$" x $\frac{3}{4}$" x $21\frac{3}{4}$" each

MATERIAL LIST:
One 8' piece of 1" x 8' lumber (for front and back pieces and entry restriction)
One 5' piece of 2" x 2" lumber (for sides and ceiling)
One 3' piece of 1" x 4" lumber (roof and back extension for landing area)
One piece $15\frac{1}{2}$ x 27" fiberglass window screening. *Must be plastic screening, not aluminum!*
20-30 $1\frac{5}{8}$" drywall screws
1 pint latex acrylic paint
$\frac{5}{16}$" staples
SEE PREVIOUS PAGE FOR PLACEMENT INSTRUCTIONS
Caulking is important—make sure you caulk before screwing together so you make an airtight container.

Crandall- the bat

In Jackson Hole bats are common, but they are not commonly seen. So I was interested when told that a bat was found walking around the floor of a log cabin. What I saw was a little brown bat (Myotis lucifugus) struggling to get out of everyone's way. Wearing leather gloves I inspected the bat and found that she had a broken forearm. Bats are very good flyers but flight is still dangerous, and they occasionally make mistakes. This one must have run into the ceiling fan that was running in the building.

I didn't know what to do, but wanting to learn more I decided not to throw her out in the yard for weasel food. After talking to several zoos I had a recipe for "bat glop," a mixture of cream cheese, sour cream and banana mashed together, and instructions on how to get her to drink water from an eye dropper. She ate and drank like there was no tomorrow. Whenever I came into the room she was anxious for more. This still didn't solve the problem of her broken arm. I had heard about a vet in town who was interested in wildlife and experienced in bird orthopedics. When I called Dan Foreman at his animal hospital late one day and told him about the injury, he jumped at the chance to help. He arranged for the smallest pins to be shipped overnight for our eight o'clock appointment the next morning. When Dan excitedly asked to see the bat after I walked in, I opened my palm and exposed an animal weighing less than a sheet of typing paper and only an inch long. I remember the expression on his face as one of astonishment as he said, "I had no idea she was that small!"

This little brown bat, injured and unable to fly, is echolocating on the camera by emitting high frequency sounds through her mouth. Bats require different environmental conditions than humans and therefore do not make good pets. A wild bat should never by picked up or handled.
(Photo by Patrick Matheny)

The pins were as large as the bone to be repaired. They clearly would not work.

Dan informed his entire staff about the procedure and the operating room was full. People even came in on their day off to see surgery on a bat. Two hours later the bone had been fixed using the end of a hypodermic needle and the bat was awake and active. Her bone was stabilized but she would never fly again. The thing that impressed me most was the attitude of the staff. By the time Dan was finished and the bat was crawling around, everyone in the room had been compeletley taken in by this little creature. The usual feelings of revulsion at the sight of a bat had been replaced with an attitude of wonder and respect. Over the next six weeks during checkups she built up quite a fan club. Whenever I brought her in there was a group of people waiting to see her. Over the next year I showed her during talks I presented on bats, and I don't recall a single person, child or adult, who wasn't completely beguiled by her.

On a visit to Dan's clinic, and after the bandages had been removed for the last time, I confided to him that I was a little worried at first when I called him. I was afraid I would be told to just step on it, it was only a bat. He responded, "Well, now you know you won't hear that here."

Tom Haraden
Grand Teton National Park, Moose, WY

CHAPTER FIFTEEN

Bison

Like other mammal species that have experienced near-extermination and are now coming back, the bison doesn't fit into established wildlife management practice. Wild bison populations are limited now to Yellowstone and Grand Teton National Parks, but a steadily increasing population is causing these animals to

disperse into neighboring ranches and residential areas. Most people welcome the sight of a wild bison, but there are some concerns when bison come in contact with agricultural activities.

Bison are large, powerful grazing mammals that are unperturbed by about everything but a charging grizzly. They dominate horses, cattle, elk, deer, and even moose. They have a habit of "wallowing," or rolling on the ground, usually in a dry, dusty area to scratch their dry skin and remove old hair. Bison also rub themselves on trees, rocks, fenceposts, and poles to alleviate an itch or skin irritation. They can strip the bark from a tree, break limbs, and uproot shrubs, so trees should be protected with individual fences if bison continue to visit. They prefer the rough bark of pine trees. They dislike loud noises, and bison will charge unpredictably and can be extremely dangerous.

Bison move between winter and summer ranges. Cows, calves, and young bulls stay in a loosely formed herd, but bulls may wander alone or in small groups. Most contact with residential areas comes either in winter or while moving back to summering grounds.

BISON
RANGE
Bison bison

Bison usually travel in a slow-moving, near-sighted fashion and are oblivious to fences and roads until they come upon them. Although they appear to wander aimlessly much of the time, they have been observed making long, perfectly straight marches across open prairie to food or water. Bison can jump surprisingly well but often prefer to push through a fence with their massive head and shoulders. If you live near bison you can lower fences where possible or provide let-downs. (*See Fences, p. 32*) Bison can entangle themselves in barbed wire as they push through, dragging the strands of wire until it binds and traps them.

Bison are well suited to finding grass under deep snow and should be left to forage on their own, but they readily adapt to hay as food and are beginning to compete in winter with elk and horses for agricultural feed. This contact is of particular concern to cattle ranchers since bison may carry brucellosis, an abortion-inducing disease, although there are no recorded instances of the disease actually being transmitted to livestock from bison. (*See brucellosis, p. 63*)

A Bison Encounter

Tom Rush reported a wounded bison to National Park Service rangers when it first appeared in his remote neighborhood one fall. Tom lives on formerly private property now leased from the park service, and the house sits along a wide and erratic seasonal path of a small herd of migrating bison. The injured bison was not using its front right leg. After looking at the animal through binoculars the rangers determined it was not a human-caused injury and decided to "let nature take its course." Unfortunately, "nature's course" meant that the one-ton animal would probably die in Tom's yard, and the unhealthy bison already smelled bad.

The rest of the herd continued on to their wintering grounds, but the crippled bull was unable to travel and stayed behind in the aspens surrounding Tom's home. The snows deepened, and as the bison began to find less food it gradually got weaker and weaker. It became apparent that the bull was trapped and would most likely die in the yard. The bison kept the snow in one small area packed down and he stayed there, foraging for what he could. It was the only place the bison was aggressive.

When the bison's ribs protruded, Tom's only neighbor decided he had seen enough. He checked with a veterinarian on what to feed the bison and purchased some alfalfa pellets used for elk and deer. When those were gone he spread out supplemental hay to help keep the bison alive until the snow melted. Tom watched this activity with mixed feelings, knowing it was both illegal and contrary to the advice of wildlife biologists, but in addition to his compassion for the animal he didn't want it to die in his front yard.

The bison slowly gained weight and its wounds healed, but the injured leg wasn't improving enough to use more than occasionally. Its hoof pointed straight down. The animal became accustomed to being fed and would approach whoever was walking past its area. Tom looked for the bison every time he left his house and made detours to avoid disturbing it,

but he would occasionally take a closer look to see if the animal was sick or dying. During one of these periodic checks Tom got a little too close and the bison reacted and made a slow, three-legged charge. Tom thought the bison was just demanding food and going to butt weakly against him, but he suddenly found himself lifted up and thrown high in the air over the bison's back. He landed face down in the snow, dazed, and looked around for the bison so he wouldn't get gored again. He saw the bison a good distance away and it took a moment to realize that he had been thrown nearly thirty feet. He said it felt like he had been punched in the stomach, but when he got up he found a gash in his side where the bison had gored him. Fortunately, the other horn had hit Tom's wallet and the force was absorbed by his American Express card.

Then the most difficult part of the situation began. While his friend Renee was speeding Tom to the hospital, a state trooper pulled along, and Renee yelled over that there had been a bison goring. The trooper went ahead to lead the way, and he radioed the hospital that a man gored by a bison was coming in. The newspapers heard it on their police scanners and they arrived at the hospital soon after Tom.

His wound required stitches, a hospital stay, and a lot of explaining. By keeping mum and trying not to implicate his neighbor, Tom inadvertently gave the press something to do during a slow period, and they got as much mileage as they could from the incident. Then Tom's friends began arriving in his room to add to his embarrassment; one friend arrived wearing a red cape and carrying a sword. In the end Tom's neighbor was fined for illegally feeding wildlife, the bison survived to wander off in the spring, and Tom had a story with a moral to tell. When he returned home Tom measured the distance from where the bison had gored him to where he had landed in the snow: twenty-six feet.

C.C.

Brucellosis:
The bacterial disease

Among the many diseases transmittable from wildlife to humans or to domestic animals, the bacterial disease brucellosis has gained some sort of notoriety. It has stirred controversy over the management of wildlife, especially bison, and the relationship between wildlife and agricultural animals. Discussions of brucellosis quickly get down to basic issues of management.

Mammals, including humans, can become infected, but brucellosis is best known for its effects on cattle. It causes spontaneous abortions in the last half of pregnancy, still births, and may cause sterility in both cows and bulls. Not all calves die, and the survivors build an immunity to the disease. Later pregnancies may be normal. In 1917, bison in Yellowstone National Park were the first wild animals in which the disease was detected, but it was not known if they naturally harbored the disease or were infected by nearby cattle. The disease was then also found in the elk of Yellowstone, but only in very few deer, antelope, or elk in the rest of Wyoming.

In 1934 a program to inoculate domestic cattle and eradicate the disease was begun. It was not until the constant pressure of expanding civilization and development reached into the last strongholds of wildlife that the disease became an issue again.

Brucellosis requires some effort to be transmitted from one animal to another, ideally in close confinement of herds of animals over a long period of time. Direct contact with bodily fluids of infected animals, with stillborn calves, or placental material is needed to transmit the disease. There are no documented cases of brucellosis being transmitted from bison or elk to domestic cattle, but experiments have shown it is possible if they mingle during the birthing season.

The bison herds of Yellowstone and the elk of both Yellowstone and Jackson Hole offer perfect conditions for spread of the disease. Residential and agricultural development on land surrounding Yellowstone and the National Elk Refuge in Jackson Hole has limited the range and movement of the animals and restricted their migrations. In addition, the slow creep of development has brought cattle closer and closer to the refuges. To this is added the increasing populations of elk and bison brought about by mild winters, supplemental feeding programs and a lack of natural predators. The elk and bison remain confined in large herds much of the year because there is nowhere else for them to go, and the disease persists. Brucellosis is present in all herds of elk fed on feedgrounds, but not in herds that winter in the wild. The natural instinct for the bison and elk is to disperse, to wander away and break up the herds, but that only takes them into ranches, homesites, and direct contact with cattle.

A close association between wild and domestic animals occurs in winter when both share habitat.

Pets and Wildlife

In contrast to the confines of city or suburban life, small towns and agricultural or resort areas offer the space needed for pets like large dogs, cats, and a few more exotic species. But often that open space is wildlife habitat, and pets that are allowed to roam out of the house and yard can come in conflict with wildlife.

Occasionally pets can be the victims of these encounters, but more often it is the wildlife that loses.

DOGS: Sport and guard dogs are popular pets where there is room for them to run in the open spaces of large plot developments and small acreage parcels. Much of this development occurs on land bordering agricultural fields, along the foothills and on wooded hillsides—all prime year-round wildlife habitat and critical wintering grounds.

While many dogs are highly trained and controlled, others are family pets and are allowed to come and go as they please. When exercising your dog along trails or back roads, remember that you are passing through the home territories of various wildlife species. Keep to the trails and give any wildlife a wide berth.

Certain breeds of dogs have been bred to hunt large mammals or birds or to help control rodents, and most of those hunting instincts remain even when the dog isn't used for these purposes. Neighborhood dogs allowed to run loose inevitably form packs from two to a dozen or more and the hunting mentality sets in. Many pet owners would be surprised to see their gentle Labrador retriever side by side with the neighbor's dogs in hot pursuit of a deer foundering in deep snow.

Winter is the most critical time for dogs to be controlled. Wildlife, especially deer, become confined to small areas and are often subsisting on marginal food sources. A deer that could easily outrun several fat dogs any other time of year can quickly exhaust itself in deep snow. Under certain snow conditions dogs are able to run on the surface while deer break through, making them even more vulnerable. Winter trails, roads and packed migration paths become traps for the deer.

Fenced yards and large pens, enclosed runs, or cable "dog runs" all give a dog adequate space while unwatched. Dogs restrained in mountain lion or bear country need to be protected with completely enclosed kennels. Once the dog is free it needs to be controlled if wildlife appears. "Invisible fences," or radio controlled shock collars, are very effective for keeping dogs within a certain perimeter. These methods also make them more effective guard dogs and keep unwanted wildlife from entering the yard to feed on landscape vegetation. Ideally, pets should be restrained throughout the year.

CATS: A study done in England on predation by domestic cats upon songbirds revealed a phenomenal number of birds killed each day, many more than the cat owners were aware of. Cats allowed to roam will kill songbirds as well as mice, particularly in the nesting season and in winter when the birds are concentrated around bird feeders. Probably the most effective means of controlling cats outdoors is to fit them with bells or other noise-making devices that will alert birds.

WILDLIFE VS PETS: Wild animals are not afforded the luxury of free meals and a warm home, and they live under much more rigorous and competitive circumstances than domestic animals. They are generally faster, stronger, and more skilled at fighting and defending themselves than pets. Domestic pets caught alone by predatory wildlife are usually killed or badly injured.

COYOTES AND PETS: Each year a number of cats and dogs fall prey to coyotes. Coyotes are skilled hunters, working in pairs or teams, and their taunting often lures dogs out to be killed and eaten. Late winter and early spring are times when natural food is scarce and coyotes are hungry and more likely to attempt to kill dogs. Restrain your dog when it wants to chase barking and yipping coyotes. Hungry coyotes have even snatched pets off the back porch, so extra care must be taken during the lean months.

MOOSE AND PETS: Unlike deer, a grown moose is more than a match for a dog. Moose are aggressive and will not only defend themselves but will pursue whatever is bothering them. Their powerful front feet and sharp hooves can quickly kill a large dog.

PORCUPINES AND PETS: Porcupines almost always win in encounters with dogs, unless the dog is a skilled and experienced killer. A porcupine will consider any dog, even a playful puppy, to be a threat. Porcupines cannot throw or shoot quills but will lash out with their powerful, quill-covered tail. Porcupine quills can cripple or even kill a dog if not treated. Most encounters by inexperienced dogs involve so many quills that a trip to the vet is necessary. Individual quills can be removed by a quick yank of the pliers, although the barbed structure of the quill tears tissue on the way out and infection can occur. Some dog owners say that dogs learn to avoid porcupines if they are not anesthetized for the removal of the quills, but this is a very painful process and its usefulness as a learning experience is doubtful. Some dogs become obsessed with porcupines, viciously attacking the source of their pain in spite of the damage they receive. These individual dogs need to be removed and placed in homes far from porcupine habitat.

SKUNKS AND PETS: Skunks are usually more of a problem to pet owners than to the pets themselves. A skunk's defensive spraying ends the pursuit and prevents bites or wounds to pets, except in cases where the skunk is diseased, as with rabies. *(See Rabies, p. 66 and Skunks p. 54)*

RELEASING PETS: Releasing any pet into the wild is cruel and unfair to both the pet and the wildlife inhabiting the release area. Feral dogs often form vicious packs, and cats survive on their own by killing whatever they can.

Any pet, particularly exotic ones that may carry diseases or have an unfair advantage over indigenous wild species, should remain in captivity rather than being released to fend for themselves. Unwanted pets should be placed in new homes, given to an animal shelter, or humanely put to sleep.

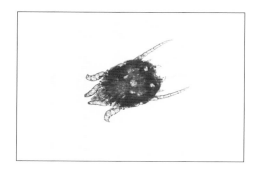

Diseases and Parasites

Wild animals are not regulated and inspected like livestock and are not inoculated against disease. They are subject to a number of parasites, infections, and diseases that appear at various times of the year under differing circumstances. The bacterial or viral agents are always present in some small percentage of the

population but remain benign. Most outbreaks of disease occur naturally as a result of seasonal changes in the condition of the animals. Healthy animals normally recover while the weaker ones die and the disease disappears. In cases where animals are crowded or stressed due to human pressure, the effects of the disease are magnified and entire herds can suffer.

Bighorn sheep provide a prime example of the magnifying effects of reduced habitat and crowding on the incidence of disease. These wild sheep suffer from a parasite called lungworm, which spends the adult part of its life in the lungs of sheep. Eggs are laid and hatched in the lungs and the larvae travel up the trachea, are swallowed, and pass out of the animal. The larvae then penetrate the soft feet of terrestrial snails and moult into an infectious stage. As sheep graze they inadvertently eat the small snails, the larvae migrate to the lungs, and the cycle begins again.

Normally the lungworms pass through the sheep without really harming them and the sheep move on to graze on uninfected grass.

When bighorn sheep are confined to smaller and smaller ranges and are forced to compete for limited food with domestic sheep and cattle, as well as other wildlife like elk and deer, they overgraze and continually recycle the lungworms. The accumulative infestation of lungworms causes severe pneumonia, and entire herds can be wiped out.

Most wildlife diseases and parasites remain in the wild populations, but a few are carried over into domestic animals and livestock. The reverse is less common since most pets and livestock receive inoculations and do not carry disease. Here are some of the concerns when living around wildlife.

DISEASES TRANSMITTABLE TO HUMANS FROM WILDLIFE

RABIES: Rabies is an acute, fatal disease caused by a virus. It causes mental disturbance, behavior changes, paralysis, and death. The rabies virus is carried in saliva and is usually transmitted by a bite from an infected animal. It is also passed to cuts and scratches when carelessly handling an animal, alive or dead. Domestic pets are required to have vaccinations against rabies, so most cases of the disease involve wild animals. Foxes, skunks, bats, raccoons, coyotes, and other mammals can be infected.

Any wild animal that appears sick, overly friendly, or excitable should be avoided and wildlife officials contacted. Bites to humans often occur when attempting to help or feed sick looking, weak, or partially paralyzed wildlife. A veterinarian must have the body of the animal to determine if it has the disease.

TULAREMIA: Tularemia, often called "rabbit fever," is a bacterial disease of rabbits and other mammals, usually passed through a cut or scratch. It is often contracted by handling an infected animal with bare hands, especially by hunters who come in contact with animal blood. Tularemia is also transmitted by ticks and biting flies. It is more common in late summer and early fall. Visible symptoms in animals include weakness and apparent tameness, and an overall appearance of poor health. It is most often carried by the Rocky Mountain wood tick and the American dog tick.

BUBONIC PLAGUE: The plague is a bacterial disease that persists in rodent populations and makes occasional outbreaks into the human population. In the past, before treatment was developed, it was responsible for large epidemics. The plague is transmitted to humans via the fleas of infected rodents. Rats and ground squirrels are both carriers of the disease. Rodents nearly always have fleas, so precautions should be used when handling them. Do not reach into burrows, and do not handle dead rodents without wearing gloves.

ROCKY MOUNTAIN SPOTTED FEVER: Related to typhus and tick fever, Rocky Mountain spotted fever is dangerous and often fatal. Spotted fever is transmitted by ticks, with the reservoir of disease in various ground squirrel species. Once a tick feeds on an infected ground squirrel it may drop off and re-attach to another mammal and may carry the disease miles from the reservoir of infection. An infected female tick may lay several thousand eggs which will develop into infected larval ticks, and any stage can transmit the disease. Care should be taken to check for ticks during tick season (spring and early summer) and also to check pets, especially dogs. (*See Ticks, p. 66*) There are no noticeable symptoms in diseased rodents, but one of the first symptoms for humans is a rash of bruise-colored spots on the soles of the feet, ankles, palms, and wrists. If untreated, within a week it may progress to coma.

LYME DISEASE: Lyme disease is caused by a bacterium commonly found in deer blood and historically has not been a problem. However, recent increases in deer populations around inhabited areas have made exposure to the disease more likely. Once limited to the northeast United States, Lyme disease has now been reported in most states. The disease is transmitted by a tick that has fed on an infected deer, and tick populations increase along with the deer numbers. Large numbers of deer combined with more interest in hiking and enjoying the outdoors contribute to the rise of incidents. Lyme disease goes through three stages: first, a rash and flu-like symptoms; second, anywhere from a week to months later, headaches, paralysis, numbness, or meningitis; months or even years later comes the third stage consisting of arthritis, fatigue, and loss of memory.

HANTAVIRUS: Hantaviruses are a source of sickness carried by rodents. They are found primarily in Asia where they cause periodic outbreaks of disease. In North America the hantavirus is carried by the deer mouse, *Peromyscus maniculatus*. Each rodent species carries a different virus. Although our hantavirus is primarily found in deer mice of the southwestern states it has been reported in almost every state.

Hantavirus causes severe flu-like symptoms that progress rapidly to death caused by fluid-filled lungs. It appears to be an over-reaction by the body's immune system that causes death, since very young and very old patients with weaker immune systems often recover.

Hantavirus is found in mouse urine and feces. The virus is inhaled when mouse nests or dead mice are handled or infected areas are disturbed. Dead deer mice and mouse traps should be handled only with gloves. Traps, nests, piles of feces, urine, and dead mice can be saturated with chlorine bleach to kill the virus. Although the odds of being infected with hantavirus are small, it is wise to treat all deer mice as carriers. Sweeping, dusting and cleaning in areas used by deer mice seem to be the prime means of stirring up virus-laden feces and dried urine.

TUBERCULOSIS: Tuberculosis is a bacterial infection that progresses like a slow-motion hantavirus. Although it is well controlled in the United States the disease is still found in some wildlife species, particularly in Montana.

DISEASES ARE TRANSMITTED FROM INFECTED WILDLIFE TO HUMANS THROUGH TWO MAIN BITING PARASITES:

TICKS: Ticks are arachnids, related to spiders, scorpions, and mites. They survive by sucking blood from their warm-blooded hosts. A tick has a small head and a barbed mouth with a sharp sucking appendage like a straw. The barbed mouth holds on while the sucker cuts into blood vessels. The tick's saliva contains an anticoagulant to keep the blood from clotting while it sucks up blood into its main body, which may expand to fifty times its normal size. When the tick is full it will drop off.

Ticks go through stages of egg, larva, nymph, and adult. Larvae have six legs, and nymphs and adults have eight legs. Except for the eggs, all stages attach to a host and suck blood. Ticks can sense carbon dioxide, a product of respiration in warm-blooded animals, and they crawl toward it. There are various species of ticks, but the American dog tick, the Rocky Mountain wood tick, and the deer tick are the most common.

To reduce the chances of getting a tick bite you should wear light colored clothing so the ticks are more visible, check your body each day, check your pets, and wear tick or insect repellent when hiking or working in woods and brush. Wear long pants and tuck the pantlegs into your socks.

TO REMOVE A TICK: Ticks don't latch on as soon as they crawl onto skin and may take a while to really attach themselves. The best way to remove one is to use tweezers or blunt forceps to grab the tick as close to your skin as possible and pull it gently and steadily away. Don't crush or squeeze the body. Kill the tick by dropping it in alcohol or flushing it down a toilet, and disinfect the bite with alcohol. If disease is a concern you should save the tick in a small vial so it can be used to confirm any symptoms you may develop.

FLEAS: Fleas are small wingless insects that live as parasites on animals. They feed on blood, lay eggs and go through stages similar to a tick. They can occur by the thousands on larger mammals and are notorious for their jumping ability. Anyone who has approached a badly infested dog is aware of the speed with which they can transfer hosts. Fleas are carriers of disease, notably the plague, and pass the disease by biting new hosts. Most fleas reach humans through pets or by indiscriminate handling of wild animals. Fleas can often be observed abandoning the body of a rodent caught in a

trap or hit by a car as the body cools off.

There is a great variety of fleas, each specializing in one host, but they often cross over and carry their diseases with them. Species include the rat flea, dog flea, cat flea, human flea, carnivore flea (on bears and wolves, etc), the bat flea, rodent flea, bird flea, and mouse flea.

The best prevention is to treat pets regularly for fleas and fit them with flea collars if possible. Don't handle any dead wildlife, especially rodents, until the body has cooled off for several hours and then wear gloves and watch for fleas. Treat dog and cat beds and any other pet that may contact wild animals. Don't reach into any animal burrows.

CHAPTER EIGHTEEN

Wetlands and Waterways

A wetland is any area with shallow standing water most of the year, boggy or swampy ground, or a marsh. Wetlands are the transition between dry land and open water. These areas are critical not only for the species that live and reproduce there, but also for all those species dependent on wetlands as a food base, including humans. Wetlands cleanse flowing water and recharge aquifers, control flooding and provide nutrients. Many of the native wetland species exist nowhere else.

Of all the types of habitat likely to be found near private homes, wetlands are the most fragile and most easily destroyed during home or road construction. They are also the most beneficial to a healthy diversity of wildlife and should be protected. Anyone lucky enough to live along a waterway or next to an area of wetlands has a special responsibility to that critical land.

Wetlands are fragile, and disruptions like roadways, bridges, culverts, and livestock can damage the soil and vegetation. Any diversion of the natural flow of water reduces the capacity of the wetlands to function as a means of flood control. If you have wetlands on your property, put on a pair of hipboots and explore it some time. If it isn't attractive to you there are a number of things you can do without draining the land or altering its ecological function.

Wetlands are generally easy places to grow willow, alder, and cottonwoods, all attractive to moose, deer, and birds. Native species do best, and through thinning and creative planting you can build a beautiful oasis for both migrating and resident wildlife. Include viewing spots or canoe paths, and enjoy it even more. A marshy area is a great place to provide nesting boxes, perching poles, and nesting islands.

Wetlands and the wildlife using them change with the seasons. Summer may find open water with waterfowl, moose submerging their heads for aquatic vegetation, and bats flitting over the surface at dusk. The middle of winter may see the water and ground frozen solid and covered with snow. A herd of deer might browse on willows and waxwings feed on the last few berries.

PLANT SPECIES FOR WETLANDS: Plant water-tolerant species like alder, willow, and birch to provide cover for wildlife. One good thing about wetland plantings is that they don't really need any care. Berry-producing plants like silverberry, elderberry, raspberry or chokecherry tolerate a lot of water and can be planted around the edges to provide food for wildlife. Cattails, reeds, sedges, and pond lilies can all be seeded to provide a richer environment.

Remember that a permit is required from the U.S. Army Corps of Engineers before any wetland can be modified. This includes "improvements" to the wetland.

Great Blue Heron

WATERWAYS include all sorts of creeks, ponds, irrigation ditches, rivers, and lakes. They often begin or end in wetlands. Sometimes a residential development is incorporated into former agricultural land or portions of it. In these cases there are often irrigation ditches that provide seasonal water. Ditches are ideal for planting cottonwoods, willows, spruces, and other native, water-tolerant trees. This streamside vegetation creates nesting habitat for many songbirds like warblers, hummingbirds, and thrushes.

Widen a spot or two in a ditch even if you can't create a seasonal pond fed by the irrigation water. Water attracts wildlife if it is accessible, shallow, and there is some vegetation along it.

Properly managed creeks and rivers can provide good habitat for fish as well as birds, insects and small mammals. As with any other habitat, providing variety with lots of cover and food is the key to attracting and keeping wildlife. (*See Landscaping, p. 86*)

Ponds are popular ways of inviting wildlife onto your property. Instead of digging a deep pond and filling it with one species of non-native fish, you can leave one bank shallow for feeding waterfowl, plant one section with thick vegetation for birds and insects, and build an island to attract nesting waterfowl. You can stock a variety of native fish species, including minnows and other important food species for wildlife, but you should first check with your state Game and Fish agency for permits to stock fish.

Think Globally

Biodiversity is simply a term for all the variety of life that has evolved on earth, from algae and ants to mule deer and moose. Biodiversity is not just the end result of millions of years of evolution; it is the foundation for continuing the miraculous process of life. In this case, variety is not only the spice of life, it is a key ingredient.

A decline in biodiversity may not seem too critical to us. We fight to save a few endangered species and occasionally bring animals back from the brink of extinction, but life in general goes on. Unfortunately it is not the animals which we see every day that are of concern to biologists, not the deer or the squirrels or the swans. It is not even the more exotic things in the world like gorillas and zebras. The critical element in maintaining biodiversity, and thus life, is habitat. It is native plants, forests, wetlands, grassland.

While we as homeowners and property owners often feel far removed and somewhat helpless in issues like the fight against clearcutting tropical rain forests, there is something we can do locally to maintain biodiversity. The effort begins at home, with the preservation of land in its natural state. If a portion of a building lot is left in native vegetation, and all the lots of a development do the same in some connected fashion, a large piece of native land will be intact. If the trees and grass remain, if the fungus in the soil and the insects and bacteria are all in place, then the songbirds and deer will have a better chance to survive.

A Fall From Grace

What started off as a quick trip to the local market for some last minute dinner ingredients turned out to be a gut-wrenching episode I was not soon to forget. It was late afternoon and I was driving north on the Teton Village Road admiring the expansive view of the snow covered Tetons. As if this picture was not perfect enough, six trumpeter swans flew into view. These large white birds painted against a white landscape was almost surreal. The breath-taking grace of these birds sailing through the air was suddenly broken when one bird tumbled from the air. The others made quick turns to the right and left to avoid the deadly powerlines strung across their path in the sky.

I quickly pulled over to find the fallen swan alive and running awkwardly towards the road. Leaping from the car I signaled the oncoming traffic to stop while the large white bird crossed the road heading in the direction the birds had been flying from. The bird was stopped quickly by a fence running parallel to the road. Trapped between the road and the fence all I could do was keep this beautiful creature from coming back into the road while another onlooker went to call the Wyoming Game and Fish Department for help.

When the local swan biologist arrived at the scene the swan made a desperate attempt to escape. We all watched helplessly as it became airborne and flew along the roadway gaining altitude ever so slowly. It was able to avoid the cars heading up the roadway then banked to the left at tree level but failed to clear the powerlines again. It died as a result of this final impact with the lines.

I could barely see driving home, my eyes so filled with tears and my heart filled with a heaviness hard to describe. The image was hard to dispel from my thoughts and haunted me for months. That memory has fueled an effort to reduce a frightfully high number of these beautiful birds being killed by power lines and fences in my county. The Jackson Hole Wildlife Foundation, working closely with the Wyoming Game and Fish Department and our local utility company and private landowners, has made significant strides in visually marking powerlines and either taking down or marking fence crossings of waterways used by swans.

In the days after the accident I noticed five swans flying over the area numerous times. Swans mate for life and I often wonder if they were all trying to find their fallen friend and for how long they would look.

By Meredith Campbell, founder of Jackson Hole Wildlife Foundation

CHAPTER NINETEEN

Beaver and Muskrats

Beavers are big, reddish brown rodents with a large, flat, and scaled tail. When wet they appear almost black. Beavers live in and around water, and are mostly nocturnal, but may be seen in daylight when preparing for winter. In general they are associated with ponds, rivers, and streams with enough water to give

them protection. If the water isn't deep enough to suit them, beavers will build the dams for which they are so well known. Dammed streams give the beaver a protected place to build a lodge, provide water deep enough not to freeze in winter, and give access to surrounding vegetation. Along rivers and lakes beavers do not build dams but make burrows in the bank. They eat the bark of trees, twigs, and aquatic vegetation. They breed in midwinter and give birth in the spring. Beavers are believed to mate for life.

Beaver ponds are tremendously rich wildlife habitat. From microorganisms in the mud to insects, trout, ducks, frogs, moose, and swans, the ponds offer a diversity rarely found in such a small space.

BEAVERS ON THE PROPERTY: If a single beaver or a beaver family moves into the neighborhood it's unmistakable. As they are nocturnal, you may not actually see the beaver, but fallen trees, gnawed limbs, and a dam across running water are obvious signs.

BEAVER
RANGE

Castor canadensis

Around a pond or along a stream you may find muddy trails leading from the water into the vegetation or stubs of neatly chewed off willows, aspen or cottonwood branches with the bark gnawed away.

ENCOURAGING BEAVERS: Beavers are interesting neighbors on larger bodies of water and around wetland areas. The ponds they create are magnets for waterfowl and other birds, moose, deer, and fish. Over the years an established beaver pond fills in with sediment and the beaver moves on, leaving behind an eventual meadow. If you want the beavers to stay, some help in the way of keeping the pond open may be required. Planting willow shoots along the banks each year will help ensure a regular food source.

DISCOURAGING BEAVERS: Frequently beaver are unwelcome visitors and are especially bothersome when damming irrigation ditches and small streams, flooding

roads and yards and cutting down trees. They are fast and persistent workers and not easily discouraged. Destroying the dam only seems to make them work harder. They are also good at digging tunnels and may undermine roads and collapse banks. They can easily cut down and haul away small ornamental trees in one night, and larger trees can be girdled and killed even if not felled. Since beaver hide by day in lodges, burrows and tunnels, they can be hard to remove. They can be live-trapped and transferred by an experienced trapper. If the beaver and their dams are desired, dams can be perforated with drain pipes to match the

lack of food or water will discourage them, so if the water source can be closed down or diverted the beaver will move on. Planting spruce and pine trees, not ideal fare, will prevent beavers from eating in certain areas.

Beavers often dam up culverts beneath roadways. Commercial structures, like steel mesh cylinders that fit over the end of the culvert, are available to help prevent this.

MUSKRATS: Muskrats are often associated with beavers and beaver dams, although they are also found on their own. They require less water, living in marshy areas or along the shores of a stream or pond. They do not build dams, but they do build cone-shaped lodges of mud and grass. Young beavers and muskrats can be mistaken for each other, especially when swimming, although the muskrat has smaller features and quicker movements. Muskrats have big heads and a long, vertically flat tail and appear dark brown to black when wet and a reddish to silvery brown when dry. They eat aquatic vegetation and are fond of cattails.

Like beavers, muskrats burrow and tunnel along the shores of ponds and streams. They are not as destructive as beavers and do not cut down trees and shrubs, but they can inad-vertently drain trout ponds with their burrows. They can be trapped and removed alive, although they are sometimes trapped commercially for their fur.

M U S K R A T
R A N G E

Ondatra zibethicus

inflow and prevent flooding.

A tight, metal fence will repel beavers, but they may burrow under if it is in or near water. Individual trees can be wrapped with sheet metal at the base, or a commercial repellent may be applied to vegetation. A

CHAPTER TWENTY

Black Bear

Bears

Bears are large, omnivorous animals that have a reputation for being more carnivorous than they truly are. Most of their diet is comprised of plants, but when given the opportunity they readily prey on animals and feed on carrion. Bears are active from early spring through late fall, depending on the temperature and

snowfall, and sleep through the coldest winter months. They are not true hibernators but deep sleepers who awaken occasionally during the winter. Their seasonal nature makes them voracious feeders as soon as they leave their dens in the spring and in the fall when they are putting on fat and preparing for the winter's sleep.

Most encounters with bears around human dwellings occur when bears are attracted to the smell of garbage, cooking food, fruit, dog food, horse feed pellets and grains, bird feeders, compost, and other delicious odors. Bears are normally shy, nocturnal animals, but when natural foods become scarce they wander boldly into civilization.

BLACK BEARS VS GRIZZLIES: Most encounters around homes and ranches involve the more numerous black bear. They are found over a much wider range

than grizzlies and accommodate human presence better, even learning to exploit these situations. Except in unusually dry years when grizzlies are forced out of the backcountry by a lack of food, most bear incidents involve black bears. Grizzly bears may kill livestock on the remote edges of a ranch but are otherwise rarely seen around human development.

Because there are always exceptions to normal animal behavior, especially bear behavior, the species should be identified before you act. A large black bear may kill livestock at night and give the outward indications of being a grizzly, while a young and hungry grizzly might raid garbage cans much as a black bear would.

Black bear range in color from black to cinnamon. Their snout is generally tan, and they can have a white

BLACK BEAR
RANGE

Ursus americanus

GRIZZLY BEAR
RANGE

Ursus horribilis

blaze on the chest. Their head profile is practically a straight line from ears to nose. Some lighter colored black bears can have the appearance of being grizzled. Black bears appear to be thinner, with flat faces. Their walk is kind of an amble. They often appear awkward, but they are agile climbers.

Once you have seen a grizzly or two the differences are obvious. Grizzlies also vary in color from yellow-brown to black with white-tipped hairs, but there is a distinct hump above the front shoulders, and the profile of the face is more concave, or dish-shaped. The front claws appear to stick almost straight out. Grizzlies look more rounded, with more curves and humps. Their heads are fairly massive with rounded ears and cheeks, and the eyes can appear to be small. Grizzly cubs can climb easily, but grown bears lose that ability.

BEARS ON THE PROPERTY: Bears are smart, adaptable animals. They learn quickly, and this combined with their strength and persistence makes them successful foragers. When bears, particularly blacks, come in contact with the offerings of civilization they learn where the food is and how to get it, and they remember these lessons well. Black bears learn to bluff charge, to harass and push until they get what they want. A garbage can, beehive, fruit tree, compost pile, or barrel of oats will be visited over and over.

Bears are powerful and have an extremely good sense of smell. They will break into cars, tear down gates and doors, and climb into all manner of containers looking for the source of a good smell. It's easier to prevent them from coming in the first place than it is to break them of the habit. They have been known to climb into things

that they can't get out of, such as dumpsters.

If bears are around, garbage should be kept locked up in a garage, porch, or closed barn. The same goes for dog food, animal feed, and livestock grains. Don't leave an unoccupied house with doors or windows open. Game meat should be hung only in a locked shed or garage where it is safe. Barbeque grills need to be cleaned or burned off to eliminate scraps and drippings. Bears are so habitual they can be counted on to turn up around the same time each night, and can be frightened off with lights and loud noises, but you will have to be more persistent than the bear. A barking dog will discourage bears, but they should not be let loose to chase them. Bears have also been known to kill chained dogs.

All bears should be considered potentially dangerous and treated with great respect. While a black bear sighting is common and usually not serious, a grizzly can be unpredictable. You can often handle problems with black bears yourself, unless they become badly habituated and aggressive, but a grizzly bear should be reported to local game wardens.

BLACK BEAR SIGN: Garbage cans overturned and emptied, bags and boxes torn open, door and window trim ripped off or scratched, large piles of bear scat (large droppings often containing berries or indigestible evidence of human garbage like aluminum foil)—all these are evidence of black bears. Gardens may be torn up, branches of trees broken, and things generally turned over and pulled apart. *(See bear tracks, p.83)*

GRIZZLY BEAR SIGN: When in contact with civilization, the main sign of their presence is usually dead livestock partially eaten and covered with torn up sod, soil, and loose vegetation. Other signs include large areas of ground dug up for rodents or plant bulbs and roots, garbage scattered and trampled, large droppings containing evidence of their diet, stripped bark, and clawed or rubbed trees.

Mountain lions *(See mountain lions, p. 94)* inhabit much of grizzly country and may also cover a kill with scraped up dirt and vegetation. It may be difficult for an inexperienced observer to tell the difference. A deer is more likely to be the kill of a lion than of a bear, but the same degree of caution should be used around any predator's kill.

PEPPER SPRAY: Wildlife managers are recommending persons entering grizzly country purchase and carry on their belt at least a 15-ounce canister of pepper spray. The spray should be at least 10% *Capsicum* pepper.

Never a good scene to come home to—a black bear's sensitive nose will lead him to food smells and trouble.

Counter Assault and *Bear Prepared* are two brand names, costing from $30-50. The spray propels a wide fog which makes it more likely for the repellant to hit the target—the bear's face—than a bullet. The grizzly's ability to mutilate a hunter after being shot with a firearm is well documented.

Shed Story

It was late October, the month that turns the leaves to crunch. I huddled on the front porch of my cabin trying to read in the setting sunlight, but a southwest wind stung my face and ruffled the pages. Closing the book, I wondered how long before the bleak winds howl down Death Canyon and out over the bench overlooking the Snake River behind my cabin? How long it would take this year for blowing snow to pile over the driveway, rendering it impassable until April?

A high-pitched questioning sound interrupted my thoughts. It came from the top of the double rows of firewood which neatly enclosed most of the porch. My tabby cat Lizzie arched her back into a delicious-looking stretch and yawned, baring tiny white fangs. Digging her claws into a chunk of lodgepole pine bark, she meowed her query once again before leaping to the floor and scurrying through brittle grasses to the back of the cabin.

It was the sound of Al's truck that had piqued her curiosity. Al backed up his Ford pickup to the shed, smiling and pointing to the back of the truck. The freezer would be filled with fresh elk meat for the winter. I clapped my hands in childish relief.

He had field-dressed the elk in the woods, leaving the inner organs and the head for coyotes and ravens. I helped him haul the hind- and front quarters into the shed, where we hung them on hooks for several days of curing before butchering and packaging.

Dying glimmers of sunlight faded over Mt. Hunt as I closed the shed door. Lizzie lurked under a bare shrub and I scooped her up into my arms. She didn't fight me; she was ready for a warm fire and a good dinner as I was. Indoors, I filled her bowl with Iams. Al was already working on the dinner, and I started the fire. In an hour, we were satisfied and comfortable.

It had been a long day; we turned in early. Lizzie was especially antsy that night and prowled the house pouncing at imaginary prey. Having worked much of my life as a therapist, I strongly suspected that this cat harbored an active delusional system. She thought she was a bobcat, or even a mountain lion. Her nocturnal leaps and pounces were so disconcerting that I kept a loaded weapon on my nightstand: a water-filled spray bottle. After three well-deserved spritzes, Lizzie gave up hunting and curled up into a ball at my feet.

I listened to a clotted silence. I had never known such silence as in this log cabin in Moose, Wyoming. At night, I listened so hard for stray noises that I often heard blood coursing through my own veins. That night I heard my blood circulating.

I don't know what came first, the sting of Lizzie's claws in my feet or the abominable scratching sound. I bolted up in bed. Lizzie, a ridge of hair bristling along her spine and her tail puffed up like a raccoon's, jumped to the window sill.

The sound came from the direction of the shed, which we could not see from the window because of the angle of the cabin. Al rapped on the window with his knuckles and we squinted hard into the moonlight. The tail end of a plump black bear lumbered away from the shed and disappeared into the aspens. Lizzie arched her back and leaped into the bed, burrowing under the blankets. So much for delusions.

We ran outside. The bear had ripped a basketball-sized hole in the door of the shed. Coarse, black hairs stuck to the rough edges of the hole where its paws had groped, narrowly missing the elk meat.

Al went to work nailing plywood boards over the hole, while I stalked around the shed with flashlight and stick, beating on tree trunks, screaming obscenities and daring the bruin to return.

When the hammering ceased, I returned to the shed. "It looks like something out of *The Wizard of Id*," I said, touching several of the nail points Al had driven through the plywood facing out. We all went back to bed, Lizzie eagerly curled up in my arms.

After a while Lizzie left my arms and returned to the window sill. She stood guard at the window until faint wisps of light crept onto Sleeping Indian Mountain, but the bear did not return.

With time and its accompanying amnesia, my little cat would resume her delusions of power and dominion over the household.

By Mary Beth Baptiste

Fishing Camp Bear

Marilyn McElheney and her husband Mike were camping and fishing for the weekend and left their truck parked near a small fishing camp to hike to a nearby lake. Following the prescribed advice for bears, they put their food and garbage in a cooler inside the truck and left the doors and windows closed up tight.

When they returned from fishing they were excited to see a black bear near their truck, but then noticed debris strewn all over the ground and realized the bear had broken in. Suddenly two bears popped their heads up inside the truck and a third climbed out the other side! There had been three bear cubs in the truck. The bears had broken two windows and pushed the cooler out after emptying the contents inside the truck. They chewed up the dashboard, broke off the mirror, tore the upholstery and broke in to the glove box where they chewed up a tube of seam sealer and smeared it all over. Somehow they missed a package of pork chops. There was catsup and milk everywhere, muddy footprints all over the truck inside and out, and the bumper was ripped half off. The ground was covered with broken glass and garbage. The truck was practically destroyed.

The bears ran off and left Marilyn and Mike to inspect their truck. While they were cleaning up the mess, they noticed a clue that they had failed to see when they first arrived—the nearby fishing camp was surrounded by a massive electric fence.

C.C.

Yellowstone Grizzly

It was a gift. One of those perfect, warm, wonderful October days that can happen in Yellowstone National Park. Tom and I were setting out from the Bechler Ranger Station to camp at Boundary Creek for the last of the summer backpack/fishing trips.

Tim and Tami had been deposited with Mom for the week and we were eager to revisit Bechler, one of our past assignments in Yellowstone. The fact that after being re-assigned to Mammoth, we had left a few very large trout in the Bechler Meadows area two years earlier had something to do with our enthusiasm.

The hike that day was to be a short one, just four miles into the Boundary Creek Campground. Our backpacks were heavy with steak and potatoes for dinner—smelly perishables that had to be disposed of that first night out. I was looking forward to eating everything that might be considered a bear attractant.

About three miles along the trail, we stopped to catch my breath and had just started hiking again when I heard a terrific commotion among the thick bushes and trees off to our right. Glancing in that direction, I spotted three brown objects thundering pell-mell towards us not 40 yards away and closing rapidly. My first cry was that there were "three grizzlies running!!" Tom's first words to me were "Climb a tree!!"

Climb a tree! ! ! Easy for him to say. We had large, heavy packs and I was otherwise five months encumbered by what turned out to be our second daughter, Kelly. There was no thought in my head that I would be able to "Climb a tree." I took the only option I thought was available to protect us from that awesome threesome...I shucked my pack and tried to help Tom with his so we could defend ourselves. The only thing

I succeeded in getting off his back was the metal case protecting his fishing rod. With the case in hand, I turned to....what? Fight a female grizzly and a pair of two year old cubs? I don't know. Anyway, when I stepped from behind the tree I should have climbed, I came face to face with the most ferocious mother I have ever encountered.

She immediately reared up on her hind legs over top of me, savagely growling all the time and making the most frightening chopping sounds with her jaws. But I had a weapon! ! ! I had a metal fishing rod case! ! Oh Boy ! ! Well, I stuck that rod case into her mouth and exhorted her to "Go away, Go away." Tom vividly recalls that there was more to my language than was particularly fitting but in the heat of battle, one should not be held accountable.

She didn't go away but before she could do me harm, Tom stepped around the other side of the tree and gave her a little nudge in the side. That did it! ! ! She certainly left me alone.

Dropping on all fours, she faced this other nuisance. About ten yards away, a patch of approximately six feet tall lodgepole pine gave Tom about ten seconds of protection as that old sow chased him around that patch of trees. Realizing that she was catching up, Tom turned, crouched, and held up an arm for her to have. One mighty sweep of her foreleg tore through a suede jacket, woolen shirt, long johns, and flesh. Her claw marks were etched unforgettably in the flesh of Tom's chest. As he dropped to the ground, she reached for the first bite, unbelievably encountering his leather belt and a small amount of flesh above and below.

During those few seconds, my reaction had been to back as far away as possible from all this activity.

Encountering a log which fit my backside perfectly, I stumbled backwards and fell, feet up and belly exposed in a most compromising position.

Either our shouts back and forth to each other or her concern for her cubs confused the sow and prompted her, after downing Tom and making several false charges at each of us, to take off back down the trail looking for her twins.

To my amazement, climbing a tree when properly motivated is not that difficult. Sitting in that tree we determined that Tom's wounds were not life-threatening and tried to decide how to spend what was left of the shreds of our day.

We set up camp in the Boundary Creek Campground, laughing too loudly, stomping around too noisily, and just generally making our presence known. During that fearful night, ordinary sounds like the bugling of an elk brought me straight up out of my sleeping bag. The sounds of deer grazing in the meadow produced such a rush of adrenaline that sleep was impossible.

We decided to abandon our plans for the week's outing. The fish in the meadow held no more charm and we still had to walk back down "that trail."

Back in Mammoth, one of my good friends, in a very concerned manner, relayed to me how this type of incident could affect an unborn child and declared that she would not be surprised if my baby was born with bare feet. As intended, I interpreted that little joke as "bear feet" and for a horrified moment visualized my little baby with claws and large hairy paws.

We still frequent the woods.

By Sharlene Milligan

The Bear Called Frank

Frank Craighead studied grizzly bears for fifteen years in Yellowstone National Park. He followed them to their dens and crawled inside while they were away. He observed families and orphans and kept track of the dominant males as they fought each other. He devised radio collars for following the bears from a distance. Over the years he was chased up trees, sent running for his car and scrambling over his equipment. When he wasn't out with the bears he was studying plaster casts he'd made of their feet and teeth or listening to recordings of bear language.

So it was not surprising that nearly twenty-five years later he would look out his window early one morning to see what looked like a young grizzly standing in the yard. In the dim morning light the first thing he noticed was a big hump over the shoulders, and as the bear turned around its long, light-tipped hair caught the first rays of sunlight. What was a grizzly doing this far from its normal range in the Yellowstone and Teton Wilderness country? Then the bear turned and ambled over to the front porch and reared up to place its front

paws against the window and sniff for breakfast. It now had the distinct face and claws of a black bear. As the bear turned and dropped from the window Frank could see a great wound on one front shoulder and a crippled front foot held off the ground. It looked more like an injury from being hit by a car than from a fight with another bear. The way the bear was holding its injured foot off the ground made its shoulder push up into a hump much like a grizzly's. Its long guard hairs on the back were light colored.

The bear liked Frank's yard and stayed for several days. It grazed almost constantly on clover and slept under a spruce tree. The only incident occurred one morning when Frank was frying bacon and the bear ripped a hole in the screen door trying to get at the good smell. After a few days it was apparent the bear wasn't going to leave on its own so Park Service biologists came to tranquilize the bear and take it to a remote area. They nicknamed the bear FRANK.

C.C.

Yurt Bear

In July, 1994, I met a small black bear in an aspen draw near Rammell Mountain Road in Teton County, Idaho. I spent the summer in a tipi in these aspens. My friend, Dianne, owns a yurt on 24 acres there. I heard something approach early one evening while I was quietly reading. I stepped out to see what it was, and was surprised to see a young bear pop through the bushes. We stared at each other for a minute, both seemingly very calm. Then, as I brushed against a small aspen, she took off up the hill and out of sight.

This was one of the few times I have ever seen more than just the rear end of a bear. I figured she may have never seen a human before. She had been driven down by a severe shortage of food, as all of the bears in the Rockies had been so affected by the drought that year.

The moon and the aspens played their wonderful light game that night. I lay and watched, wondering about the bear. Would she return? Where was mamma bear? Would she tear up the tipi? Would she tear up my girlfriend on her way down the trail? A few days later, she came to visit again.

I stepped out into the glow and immediately heard a crash from the direction of Dianne's yurt. Then BAM, BAM, and the sound of a glass jar rolling across the floor. Heading to the yurt, I concluded that the little bear had hit pay dirt. The loud stomping and chomping sounds coming from inside cinched it.

Dianne had made a mistake. She had left garbage and dirty dishes in the yurt when she knew there was a bear in the area. The black bear had squeezed her way through the lattice wall after scratching a hole in the screen window. She stuck her head out the hole for a look when I started yelling for her to "GET OUT." I slammed the door a few times and walked inside. I continued to yell and the bear went over to the window. Her furry legs popped straight up as she squeezed her way out. I continued to see that familiar rear end view as I cautiously chased her back into the woods. She came right back to the yurt when I left to check on the tipi. I saw her legs pop up for the second time,

and again cautiously chased her into the woods.

This sure was an exciting way to start the day. Not ideal, however. The bear had clawed the phone line on her way in and the phone was dead. I had no way to contact Diane at work, so I cleaned up and took all the food to my car. I managed to get the radio on after fumbling with the solar system for a few minutes, and turned it up high. With the radio on, and the food out, I risked a ride to town to tell Dianne about the break in.

When we returned an hour later, there was no sign of the bear. We decided that all food and garbage would have to be stored elsewhere and left the radio on when away. Very soon, though, she encountered another human.

I jumped when the rifle cracked the next afternoon. 1, 2, 3 shots echoed through the aspens from up the road. Immediately, I wondered if the young bear was involved. The dread of it kept me from investigating. Later, Dianne stopped by to say that a small black bear had been killed for breaking into the neighbor's garage. She was after the garbage stored there. Food. An oasis in the midst of a mountain desert led her to her death. The second human she encountered killed her for eating his cast-offs.

Sorrowful questions kept coming up later. The few lame answers only brought up more questions. Was it my fault? Why would anyone be afraid of such a small bear? Why can't we store our waste in a better way? Were not WE invading HER home?

Slowly, I let the memory of her slip into the back of my mind, but vowed not to forget. She became a driving force behind my voice. A voice for the bears, a voice for all the imperiled wild things. We can't communicate, and never will with the barrel of a gun between us. So I work to convince the humans. Put down the guns, walk amidst the light of the forest, and search for the wildness within.

By Peter Leusch

CHAPTER TWENTY-ONE

Longtailed Weasel

Weasels

The weasel family, *Mustelidae,* includes not only weasels but marten, otters, mink, skunks, ferrets, and wolverines. All are fairly solitary, mainly carnivorous animals that tend to be somewhat fearless of humans. The most likely weasels to appear around dwellings are skunks, weasels and ermine, and the badger.

WEASELS AND ERMINE: There is often some confusion about weasel terminology, and the following explanation may not clear it up entirely. Weasel is a term that applies not only to all members of the Mustelidae family in general, but also to specific species like the long-tailed weasel, least weasel, or ermine. An ermine is one species of weasel that turns all white in the winter, but others, like the long-tailed weasel, also turn white in winter and are commonly referred to as ermine or winter ermine. These names are mostly interchangeable unless talking about a specific animal. If you call it a weasel you can't go wrong.

Weasels and ermine are small, long, and thin. They dart in and out of woodpiles, dive under the snow, and appear fearlessly out of nowhere. Around a home they eat chiefly mice and birds, but weasels are ferocious hunters and will kill animals as large as a rabbit or grouse. Weasels are solitary except during the breeding season and tend to stay in "home ranges" or

LONGTAILED WEASEL
RANGE

territories, so attracting them is not easy. The best you can do is to provide good habitat, which unfortunately includes mice. An old firewood pile left in a corner of the yard year-round will attract mice and eventually a weasel. Weasels are great mousers and fascinating to watch, especially as they slowly change color by shedding old fur and growing new. They also kill and eat songbirds. Weasels are fairly easy to live-trap and remove, and eliminating mice (*See Mice, p. 24*) will keep the weasels away.

MARTENS: Martens are forest-dwelling weasels about the size of a house cat. They eat chiefly mice and squirrels. Martens prefer spruce, fir, and pine forests, and are solitary animals except during the breeding season. In the wild, martens den in hollows, but around houses they are fond of attics, eaves, and other protected spaces that resemble tree hollows. A family of martens in an attic space can

Pine Marten

PINE MARTEN
RANGE

Martes americana

BADGER
RANGE

Taxidea taxus

produce incredible sounds, from rustling and scratching to a variety of vocalizations. Martens can be live-trapped and removed and the access holes sealed up with wire screen.

BADGERS: The badger is a large, burrowing weasel the size of a medium dog, about fifteen to twenty pounds, but it has short legs and a fat, wide body. The badger has a distinctive black face with a white stripe running from the nose back up over the head. Badgers feed on rodents such as gophers, mice, and ground squirrels, but will eat anything they dig up, including skunks and young coyotes.

Usually the only visible sign of a badger is a freshly excavated burrow or an area dug up and dirt scattered.

Badgers are active all year, and in winter a burrowlike opening may appear in the snow with a tailing of fresh dirt. There may be several of these together as the badger hunts for prey. Badgers are great at reducing rodent populations, especially if they find a large ground squirrel colony, but their burrowing and digging can often be more destructive than that of the rodents. Badgers can be live-trapped and removed but are unafraid of dogs or most anything else. Like all weasels badgers are fierce and vicious if cornered.

Landscaping for Wildlife

To wildlife, a new residential development springing up in the midst of their natural habitat must be a very confusing place. It may have advantages such as plowed roads in the winter with tasty salt and minerals along the shoulders and the appeal of lush ornamental vegetation. In summer there may be fresh gardens

and lawns and exotic smells. But there are also dogs and cats, cars, lights and noises, and expanses of invisible glass. Some angry homeowners throw stones while others offer sweets. There are long lines of sharp, entangling wire surrounding piles of sweet smelling, nutritious food.

For wild animals, life is an almost constant search for food. There are times of plenty, but there are also lean times when much more energy is expended than is taken in. Winter is particularly stressful on wildlife with its snow, cold temperatures, and covered food supplies. Most wild species can lose considerable body weight through the winter months but quickly regain it in the spring. It is the life they have known and they have adapted to it well. Native vegetation is the foundation of their life, and its absence, especially in winter, is life threatening.

Wild species have learned behavioral patterns which take them to areas of abundance in the winter, or at least areas of fewer natural obstacles like deep snow. These wintering grounds determine, for the most part, their population limits for the rest of the year. Unfortunately, humans recognize the same qualities in

winter habitat the animals do, and we strive to build our homes there.

Humans can distance themselves from plants, living in a more sterile setting and eating only the refined products of agriculture, but for wild animals, vegetation is life. Plants provide food, shelter, and places to attract mates and raise young. Plants and animals native to an area have evolved together to reach somewhat of a balance.

You can perhaps picture it as a multi-layered forest scene, ranging from microscopic plants on the ground up through flowers and shrubs to the upper reaches of the trees. Each plant layer has animals that utilize that layer; elk graze on the grass, deer browse on the shrubs, and birds eat the seeds. The plants have adapted to those certain kinds of use; willows browsed by deer send out more new shoots, and many seeds pass unharmed through a bird's digestive system to fall to the ground and sprout. The predators, too, have sorted out the layers and feed primarily on a certain level; the skunk hunts with its nose to the ground for insects and mice, the mountain lion stalks deer, and certain raptors like the Cooper's hawk catch small birds in mid-air.

A rural or residential yard can be pictured as a cross-section of that multi-layered forest, blocking out a space from top to bottom that will affect plants and animals at each layer. When you choose a homesite, you clear and level the ground, build a house, and then begin to landscape. What do you put back into that space?

As a homeowner you have several options depending on your feelings about wild animals and their habitats. Whether it is a herd of deer or a flock of chickadees you have moved in with, you can alter your home's natural surroundings without conflicting too much with the needs of native animals. Whichever option you choose, the best approach for wildlife is one that eliminates confusion for the animals.

OPTION 1: If you want a manicured lawn with orna-mental shrubs and exotic trees, the best thing to do is fence your yard completely with an impenetrable fence and remove it from the natural system. You can then manage birds and rodents more easily on the inside. As a concession to wildlife you can plant cover and food species outside the fence to replace some of the native vegetation you have removed.

If you want the same sculptured yard without a fence you can find native ornamental plants that are inedible or less appealing to wildlife, use organic chemical repel-lents on the vegetation, and periodically use your restrained dog or other disturbance to keep the wildlife away. This option requires considerable time and atten-tion. A cultivated lawn is held in an unnatural state of plant succession and requires considerable energy to maintain. It requires water, fertilizer, pesticides, herbi-cides, and ultimately cannot stand up to intense use by wildlife.

OPTION 2: At the other extreme, you can plant native trees and shrubs entirely and let the lawn come back in native grasses and flowers. You can open your yard to the wildlife. You can plant areas of berry- and seed-producing plants, places of thick cover, and protected openings. You can try to improve on nature and create an eden for wildlife in summer and a haven in winter.

OPTION 3: As a moderate approach, you can have a small area of cultivated lawn highlighted with native trees and shrubs that are less palatable to local wildlife. You can build an unobtrusive fence that will keep out everything but larger animals like deer and moose. You can fence individual plants in winter when you expect wildlife to show up. Organic repellents on certain plants and a dog restrained in a fenced yard will keep plant damage to a minimum. You can also give an area back to wildlife completely, planting food and cover species in a corner of the yard where wildlife can congregate.

If you take a walk through good wildlife habitat you will notice the diversity of plant species, varying both in size and density, and the mix of vegetation, open space, food plants, and cover plants. You can duplicate this to some extent in your yard, and local animal populations will adjust to utilize resources you provide.

The success of native plant growth depends on variables like elevation, soil, exposure, and rainfall. Just because a plant is found in your locality doesn't mean it will do well on your specific site.

Most state wildlife agencies can provide you with a list of native plants for your area, and local greenhouses and nurseries often cultivate native vegetation for replanting. They can also map out a landscaping plan or provide you with literature on doing so. Some areas,

Dangers to wildlife around developed areas:

Power lines and transformers.

Litter, such as plastic six-pack rings and styrofoam.

Discarded or abandoned fishing line and hooks.

Chemicals such as antifreeze, gas and oil or fertilizer.

Open barrels, buckets, cans or boxes.

Unscreened chimneys.

Careless use of pest control methods like poisons or traps.

Old wire fences, especially barbed wire, loose and in disrepair or aban-doned

Household pets—cats and dogs

such as Jackson Hole in northwestern Wyoming, have an organization devoted to the study and preservation of native plants.

NATIVE PLANTS USED FOR LANDSCAPING FOR WILDLIFE INCLUDE THREE MAIN GROUPS:

A: WILDLIFE FOOD: Grasses (such as wheatgrass and sheep fescue), berry producing shrubs (chokecherry and currant, for example) and berry producing trees such as mountain ash offer a variety of natural food.

B: WILDLIFE COVER: Shrubs such as woods rose, bitterbrush, snowbrush, and chokecherry, as well as trees (including juniper, spruce and pine) all offer protection to wildlife.

C: ORNAMENTAL: Beautiful landscaping can be accomplished with a variety of wild plants, including wildflowers such as balsamroot, lupine, and buckwheat, and shrubs such as mountain mahogany and mountain ash. Fir and maple trees are also good ornamentals. Some of these plants provide food or cover for wildlife as well. There are numerous non-native plants that are either inedible to wildlife or that provide extra food or cover.

The area covered by this book is a diverse region of mountains, valleys, canyons, and plains. Elevation, rainfall, and exposure vary considerably, often within a few miles, and the native vegetation reflects those changes. There are fingers of one habitat type projecting into another, such as small islands of forest in the prairies, or dry, open canyons in the middle of an area of lush growth. The best starting point for landscaping is to inventory what is already growing on your property and on surrounding land. Talk to your neighbors and to a local greenhouse or nursery to see what does well in your vicinity. If you are unfamiliar with the process of identifying plants, you can contact a university extension office or a state fish and game agent. Local help is often available from county agricultural offices, or from the National Park Service, the Forest Service, or the Fish and Wildlife Service.

The lists below are meant to be a starting point for selecting plants to be used as landscaping around your home. Obviously the easiest choice, in terms of success and ease of care, is to plant more of what is already growing near you. But you can manipulate things to attract or discourage wildlife, as well as to enhance the beauty of your property.

As a general rule native plants do best, require the least amount of care, and recover well from browsing by wildlife. There are also some non-native plants that actually grow faster and are hardier than the native species in addition to being low on the edibility list for wildlife. And some non-native plants have been around for so many years they are essentially native. The final selection of plants you make will be determined by your relationship with wildlife and your landscaping plans.

PREFERRED PLANTING FOR WILDLIFE
TREES FOR COVER AND ORNAMENT
Rocky Mountain Juniper, (*Juniperus scopolorum*)
Lodgepole Pine, (*Pinus contorta*)
Ponderosa Pine, (*Pinus ponderosa*)
Limber Pine, (*Pinus flexilis*)
Douglas Fir, (*Pseudotsuga menzieseii*)
Sub-alpine Fir, (*Abies lasiocarpa*)
Blue Spruce, (*Picea pungens*)
Russian Olive, (*Eleagnus angustifolia*)
Cottonwood, (*Populus* spp.)
Alder, (*Alnus* spp.)
Rocky Mountain Maple, (*Acer glabrum*)

SHRUBS FOR FOOD AND ORNAMENT:
Aspen, (*Populus tremuloides*)
Serviceberry, (*Amalanchier alnifolia*)
Siberian Pea, (*Caragana arborescens*)
Mountain Mahogany, (*Cerocarpus montanus*)
Bitterbrush, (*Purshia tridentata*)
Rabbitbrush, (*Chrysothamnus nauseosus*)
Chokecherry, (*Prunus virginiana*)
Golden Currant, (*Ribes aureum*)
Honeysuckle, (*Lonicera tatarica*)
Woods Rose, (*Rosa woodsii*)
Dwarf Birch, (*Betula glandulosa*)
Mountain Ash, (*Sorbus scopulina*)
Snowbrush, (*Ceanothus velutinus*)
Snowberry, (*Symphoricarpos* spp.)

GROUND COVER
Wooly Yarrow, (*Achillea tomentosa*)
Rockcress, (*Arabis alpina*)
Spurge, (*Euphorbia* spp.)
Stonecrop, (*Sedum* spp.)

GRASSES FOR WILDLIFE FOOD AND COVER

Western Wheatgrass, (*Elymus smithii*)
Crested Wheatgrass, (*Agropryon cristatum*)
Buffalo Grass, (*Buchloe dactyloides*)
Blue Gama, (*Bouteloua gracilis*)
Sheep Fescue, (*Festuca ovina*)

FLOWERS FOR COLOR AND WILDLIFE FOOD

Arrowleaf Balsamroot, (*Balsamorhiza sagittata*)
Penstemon, (*Penstemon* spp.)
Lupine, (*Lupinus argenteus*)
Wild Geranium, (*Geranium viscosissimum*)
Sulphur Buckwheat, (*Erigonum umbullatum*)
Sunflower, (*Helianthus annuus*)
Blue Flax, (*Linum perenne*)
Fireweed, (*Epilobium angustifolium*)

SOME PLANTS LEAST PREFERRED BY WILDLIFE AS FOOD

TREES

Birch, (*Betula* spp.)
Hawthorn, (*Crataegus* spp.)
Engelmann Spruce, (*Picea engelmanni*)
Blue Spruce, (*Picea pungens*)
Narrowleaf Cottonwood, (*Populus angustifolia*)
Douglas Fir, (*Pseudotsuga menziesii*)
Boxelder Maple, (*Acer negundo*)
Honey Locust, (*Gledistia triacanthus*)
Russian Olive, (*Eleagnus angustifolia*)
Hawthorne, (*Crataegus* spp.)

SHRUBS AND ORNAMENTALS

Red-osier Dogwood, (*Cornus sericea*)
Singleleaf Ash, (*Fraxinus anomala*)
White Dryad, (*Dryas hookeriana*)
Shrubby Cinquefoil, (*Potentilla fruticosa*)
Raspberry, (*Rubus* spp.)
Buffaloberry, (*Shepherdia canadensis*)
Creeping Mahonia, (*Mahonia repens*)
Cotoneaster, (*Cotoneaster* spp.)
Lilac, (*Syringa* spp.)
Gooseberry, (*Ribes grossularia*)
Silverberry, (*Eleagnus commutata*)

There is obviously more to landscaping than just selecting plants from a list, choosing some for food, cover, and color. Some plant species that are not browsed by deer provide important cover or food for birds or small mammals, while several good browse plants are neither pretty nor useful to other wildlife. Some non-native plant species may build extensive root systems that deprive native plants of water. The key to a successful landscaping job is diversity.

Young trees, such as aspens, are especially hard hit by browsing wildlife. You can plant older and larger trees instead of saplings or protect small trees with individual fences. You can also plant similar but less palatable trees, such as replacing aspens with cottonwoods.

If you have room on your property you can create a small wildlife haven in one corner where you provide a source of water and plant extra food and cover species. Piles of brush and clippings and trimmings from the yard make ideal wildlife cover. Logs, rocks, and thickets can attract all kinds of animals. Dripping or running water is very attractive to wildlife.

WEEDS: When you tear up the native vegetation to build a house or a road, or to trench for water or sewer, you are inviting weeds. These noxious plants, many of them introduced from overseas, thrive in disturbed soil and can quickly dominate an area, not only crowding out native plants but forcing wildlife to move in search of native forage plants. Weeds are fast growing, prolific reproducers. They resist most control methods and are largely inedible to wildlife. Hundreds of thousands of acres of habitat have been lost to weeds in the western states, and the cost of trying to control them is growing each year. Recognizing these plants, such as knapweed or Canada thistle, and getting rid of them early can eliminate having to use extensive chemical means later.

Many of the smaller weed species may go unnoticed until they have taken over and crowded out the native plants. It is important to reseed a disturbed area with native species, otherwise the exotics quickly take over. Take the time to learn which weeds are invading your locality and find out how you can help keep their numbers in check.

There is a whole science of biological control of weeds, pests and insects which you can use for more organic methods of dealing with unwanted plants and animals. Organic fatty acids have been isolated and marketed to spray or paint on plants to repel wildlife, especially deer and rabbits. Beneficial insects like ladybugs can be purchased and released to eliminate pests like aphids, and other insects are used to control plants like knapweed. There is some question about the advisability of releasing certain insects to control non-native plants. Most state Agricultural Extension Offices or county Weed and Pest Districts have information and sources for these methods.

PROTECTING YOUR INVESTMENT

Successful landscaping, especially in the cool, dry mountains can be a time consuming and expensive operation. In addition, you tend to become attached to your plants after you nurse them through droughts and snowstorms. It can be devastating to watch a herd of deer casually eat your favorite tree. There are a number of things you can do to protect your plants:

1. FENCE THE YARD: This requires a fence impassable year round to wildlife. If you like the feeling of living in a stockade, this is a good method.

2. FENCE THE INDIVIDUAL PLANT: These individual fences can be seasonal or permanent,depending on the frequency of wildlife. A few metal posts and some wire mesh will protect young trees from browsing deer, moose and elk.

3. FLASHING: Metal flashing or wire mesh wrapped around the trunk of a tree, extending up as far as possible (five or six feet) will keep deer and elk from gnawing the bark during lean winters and will deter porcupines from climbing up for a meal. Flashing the base of sapling trunks in winter will keep voles from girdling the bark beneath the snow.

4. BIODEGRADABLE CHEMICAL REPELLENTS: Nurseries and greenhouses sell a variety of products ranging from coyote urine to gooey petroleum paste, designed to discourage animals from eating your plants. You can experiment with these and other products—sometimes a product intended for one purpose works well for another. For example, pepper spray for self defense has been sprayed on trees to discourage deer, and insect trapping goo will discourage birds and mice from using openings they've made in wood siding.

5. NOISE AND LIGHTS: Irregular, intermittent noise and light will discourage animals. Unfortunately, it also disrupts your neighbors sleep.

6. RESTRAINED PETS: A barking dog, which can react to the arrival of wildlife at any time of day or night, makes a good deterrent. This requires a good leash, such as a long cable "run" or a good fence. (*See Pets, p. 64*)

WEED CONTROL NOTE:

Boiling hot water is a clean and effective weed killer for individual plants. Just use your teapot.

For larger areas, such as along a driveway, try renting a small commercial steam cleaner (used to clean car engines, etc.). The blast of steam will kill the weeds with no chemicals or pesticides.

A Word about Weeds

Many beautiful plants we admire, unfortunately, are termed "weeds" once their invasiveness is discovered. A plant that has no association to an area, a non-native or alien species, grows to a large population due to no controlling effects such as disease or bugs chewing on it. As the patch grows the weed can withstand quite severe seasonal conditions as well as becoming non-palatable to livestock and wildlife, giving it advantage over the native plants.

An introduced aggressive perennial weed called Spotted Knapweed infests 4.7 million acres of rangeland in Montana and can be found in ever increasing numbers in Wyoming. This plant has the ability to inhibit other plants from growing in the immediate area due to a chemicals produced in the weed. It also can make animals sick while foraging. Studies done in Montana show livestock carrying capacity is reduced by 80% to 90% in rangeland when Spotted Knapweed is present (Lacey, et.al, 1986). Wildlife have difficulties grazing in knapweed areas as well as in other weedy places.

In Grand Teton National Park and surrounding areas of Teton County, Wyoming there are 117 non-native species found. Furthermore, 150 non-native plants are found in Yellowstone National Park (Harvey, 1994). Each species of wildlife, like ourselves, have particular feeding habits. When a "bad apple" is thrown into the cart our choices of quality feed diminish. Likewise, the weed becomes the "bad apple" affecting wildlife foraging. Nobody escapes the demise weeds have on our fragile environment.

Our mobile society allows searching new areas and terrain, however, as we return home our bumpers, tires, boats and trailers have plant materials that would cause great destruction to our native surroundings. Keeping clean is important. As we plant our flower gardens we should pay close attention to what kinds of plants we are introducing. Some species enjoy jumping the planter box to live as a free agent. An alien plant called Dalmation Toadflax is very attractive, but is very difficult to control with current technology. This species was planted near Mammoth in Yellowstone National Park to serve as a cut flower decoration for tables in local restaurants. It has spread to at least 5,000 acres of Yellowstone Park today (Harvey, 1994).

We need to support efforts to rescue our land from threatening introductions of weed species as well as take responsibility in learning weeds and their management, especially in our own backyard. As a poster once said "Give a Weed an Inch and it will Take a Yard."

REFERENCES

Lacey, Celestine A., J.R. Lacey, T.K. Chicoine, P.K. Fay and R.A. French. 1986. *Controlling knapweed on Montana Rangeland.* Coop. Ext. Ser., Montana State Univ. Circular 311.

Harvey, Ann. 1994. *The Aliens Among Us.* Northern Rockies Conservation Cooperative, NRCC News. Vol 7.

by Fred Lamming,
Supervisor Teton County Weed and Pest

Mardy Murie's Yard

Margaret E. "Mardy" Murie grew up in Alaska in the 1920s and traveled by boat, dogsled and on foot through some of the most remote and wild land in North America. With her husband, the renowned naturalist Olaus Murie, Mardy lived among and observed grizzlies, caribou, owls, wolves, and moose. Her homes were log cabins or tents in the wilderness.

In 1927 Olaus' work took them to the frontier town of Jackson, Wyoming where they stayed to raise a family. In 1945 they bought an old dude ranch with a few log cabins set in a meadow and surrounded by spruce trees. Within a few years their home was engulfed by the expansion of Grand Teton National Park and the land surrounding them remained undeveloped.

Steller's jay

The Muries let everything grow up wild around them. A meadow of sagebrush, bitterbrush, and rabbitbrush crept in on the small patch of native grasses they called a lawn. Spruce and aspen trees cloaked the back and sides of the house, and across the meadow, a stand of cottonwoods spread along the old irrigation ditch. Alder and serviceberry grew up in thick patches. In summer the meadow was full of balsamroot and lupine.

Over the years Mardy's log cabin has almost become a natural part of the meadow. There are no salt licks and no hay bales for wildlife. There isn't a fence around the house and there's no lawnmower buzzing in the summer. Marmots, ground squirrels, chipmunks, red squirrels, and pine martens are regular summer visitors. Porcupines waddle by all year. Black bears dig for grubs in the old

Mardy Murie's cabin in Moose, Wyoming

spruce stumps and deer, elk, and moose feed in the meadow. Chickadees and jays perch behind the house and bats roost in crevices in the roof.

The winter Mardy was ninety she looked out a back window into the forest and saw a rare and beautiful lynx standing quietly at the base of a spruce tree only a few feet from her home. The lynx was undisturbed by the house, and it walked silently across a clearing and disappeared back into the wild.

C.C.

Lynx

CHAPTER TWENTY-THREE

Mountain Lion

Also called pumas or cougars, mountains lions have been slowly making a comeback since their near extermination in the late 1800s and early 1900s. For the most part mountain lions are shy, elusive animals that live in primitive and remote areas where they remain undisturbed. They are solitary except for females with

cubs or littermates that travel together. They are adaptable animals, living in a variety of habitat ranging from desert canyons to alpine forests. One of the preferred prey species of the mountain lion is mule deer, and areas with large deer populations seem to attract the cats. They also kill elk, as well as rabbits, beavers, grouse, and even porcupines.

Mountain lions are most active around dawn and dusk when the deer are moving, but they can be seen anytime of day or night. Usually you see not much more than a glimpse of a long, tan tail disappearing into the brush. You are more likely to see the sign of mountain lions than the animals themselves. Characteristic signs include partially eaten deer covered with dirt and leaves, small piles of dirt scratched up with dung and urine, and cat footprints as big as a very large dog print. A killed and eaten porcupine, with nothing left but hide and quills, is a good sign a mountain lion is nearby.

In recent years several conditions have brought about

MOUNTAIN LION
RANGE

Felis concolor

an increase in lion populations and subsequent contact with humans. Steadily rising deer populations, especially around residential areas, provide food for wandering young lions that are seeking to establish their own territories. Also, more people are moving into mountain lion habitat in new residential developments among the foothills, forests and canyons. A heightened awareness of wildlife along with a more active lifestyle that includes hiking and jogging on trails has brought about more encounters with mountain lions.

LIONS ON THE PROPERTY: If you live in known mountain lion habitat, or if you live near areas of wilderness or national forest with a plentiful deer population, there are a number of things you can do to ensure any encounter with a mountain lion will be a safe and rewarding experience.

First of all, you can help keep them at a distance by eliminating any food source. Herds of deer that gather to feed on landscaped shrubs and trees, or deer that are fed hay, are a major attraction to mountain lions. Eliminate any artificial feeding and plant only native vegetation that is unpalatable to deer if there are many deer on your property. Other potential food sources that could attract lions include garbage, dogs and cats, and livestock. All pets and livestock should be enclosed at night and pets especially not allowed to roam.

Most encounters that result in attacks on humans involve children or joggers and hikers. Mountain lions are attracted to children because of their small size and quick movements, so children in mountain lion country should be educated about the dangers and closely watched. They should be picked up and held if a lion is present. Dawn and dusk hours are critical, but a lion may be active any time of day. Joggers should avoid running in known lion habitat during these hours, if possible. Children should be supervised if outdoors late or early in the day. It also helps to clear out vegetation near yards or play areas where a lion could conceal itself.

Mountain lions, unlike bears, can be intimidated by a false appearance of size (holding a backpack above your head), loud noises, and aggressive resistance. Scream and fight back with whatever is available—a stick, rock, or backpack.

Mountain lion attacks are rare, and the chances of even seeing a wild cougar are remote. By following the basic rules for living in wildlife habitat, especially those of planting native vegetation and not feeding deer or other wildlife, you can keep lions at a safe distance.

CHAPTER TWENTY-FOUR

Raccoons

Although raccoons aren't often found in the mountainous central portion of the area covered by this book, they live on the periphery and continue to extend their range. They prefer woodlands or farmland along streams but readily adapt to urban and suburban areas. Food seems to be the limiting factor. Raccoons in the

wild are omnivorous scavengers and hunters, eating frogs, crustaceans, bird eggs, insects, fruit, nuts, and plants. The list of what they won't eat is much shorter than the list of what they will eat.

Raccoons adapt quickly to human garbage, pet food, bird seed, and compost, and it is primarily this food source that allows them to follow civilization into new territory. They can survive as long as they have a snug den and are able to gain enough weight before winter to see them through several inactive months. They do not hibernate.

Raccoons are nocturnal and their appearance in a neighborhood may be marked only by spilled garbage cans, raided vegetable gardens, and missing pet food. Once they

RACCOON

Procyon lotor

find a food source they'll return again and again, and soon become bold enough to arrive at dusk and demand food. Distinctive raccoon signs include a track showing the entire foot and all toes planted on the ground, like those of bears and humans. Garbage or compost neatly sorted out, with the undesirables placed in one pile, is another raccoon signature.

Raccoons are intelligent, inquisitive, and entertaining to observe, but they are like the ultimate bad guest who, once fed, refuses to leave. If not fed they will poke, pry, and scratch at every door and window in search of food. They will whimper, squeal, howl, churr, and scream. Their dexterous fingers make them adept at opening latches, lids, doors, and clasps. Think twice before you throw them scraps or entice them with food.

The best defense is to keep all garbage locked up, compost covered, and pet food stored away. Garbage is their chief source of food around homes. Vegetable gardens can be guarded by lights, tethered dogs, or an electric fence. Raccoons prefer to den in hollow trees but will live in abandoned burrows, culverts, barns, attics, or log piles. Holes in old buildings can be sealed, and trees or poles used for access can be wrapped at the base with a three-foot-wide band of sheet metal.

In regions where raccoons naturally occur they can be encouraged by providing stout wooden denning

FAVORITE FOODS OF RACCOONS

| Apples |
| Persimmons |
| Wild grapes |
| Acorns |
| Berries |
| Crayfish |
| Frogs |
| Minnows |
| Salamanders |
| Corn |
| Small mammals (Mice, Voles) |

boxes in wooded areas and by maintaining streams and wetlands to provide a natural food base. Unlike many other wildlife species, raccoons suffer less from the loss of habitat than from being lured into an artificial one of buildings, garbage, and handouts.

The appeal of wild animals wears off when they overstay their welcome. The raccoon will remember this window and will enter the house here if it gets the chance.

Leaving Snags for Wildlife

DEAD TREES, SNAGS, STUMPS, LOGS

They may be unattractive, but dead trees are as important to wildlife as living ones. They provide nesting sites for birds and provide well-insulated hollows for animals to survive both winter and summer temperature extremes. Insects, amphibians, birds and mammals all use dead trees and logs. Other seemingly unimportant but biologically critical lifeforms like fungi and mold need dead wood. Fallen trees in the water are invaluable to fish, birds and insects.

Any dead or dying tree that is not a hazard to property should be left intact for the wildlife. They can be trimmed or topped for safety and to reduce the chances of wind toppling them.

The metamorphosis of a solid, living tree to a hollow animal haven is fascinating to watch. Children can be introduced to this process by reading the wonderful children's book "The Hole in the Tree," by Jean George.

A growing list of products is available to assist you in furthering your knowledge that "There's Life in Dead Trees" from an organization dedicated to the preservation and protection of "Animal Inns." Their studies show that a third of all forest creatures depend on dead, dying or hollow trees for their survival, and that even fish, plants and microlife benefit from decaying wood. Only thirty bird species are capable of making their own nest cavities in trees. Another eighty animals depend upon previously excavated or natural tree holes for their nests, and are called "secondary nesters."

For more information from this organization, contact Animal Inn, P.O. Box 5065, Bend Oregon 97708-5065.

Brush Piles

Cover is one of three necessary components needed for wildlife survival. While shrubs and trees make ideal wildlife cover, they are often unavailable in many areas, require many years to become established once planted, and may not provide "optimum" habitat for ground-nesting and ground-dwelling wildlife species, even upon maturation. One alternative to provide wildlife cover is construction of brush piles or brush rows.

Brush piles for wildlife cover can be constructed quickly and easily at minimal cost and provide immediate nest, escape and winter cover for wildlife. Ideally, both permanent wildlife plantings and brush piles should be used in conjunction with one another. In the period before shrubs and trees reach optimum height for wildlife use, constructed brush piles serve a dual purpose. They act as a windbreak and trap moisture-bearing snow for the developing shrubs and trees while providing cover for wildlife. With proper location, brush piles can attract rabbits, ground-dwelling birds and many species of songbirds.

Placement, height, density of the center, and loose edges are key components to proper brush pile construction. Optimum locations for brush piles and brush rows include areas near wildlife feeding sites, along field edges, randomly scattered in overgrown or fallow fields, along upper slopes of draws and ravines, and adjacent to cultivated lands in proximity to other cover. While certain species of wildlife such as cottontail rabbits utilize much smaller brush piles, a brush pile approximately 20 feet in diameter and 3 to 8 feet in height will benefit the greatest number of wildlife species. If a lack of suitable materials or ground space prohibits construction of the optimum-sized brush pile, a smaller one is better for wildlife than none at all.

Brush piles can be constructed from a number of materials. Logs can be criss-crossed on the ground to serve as a base for the pile. Old stumps serve the same purpose with branches stacked against them. Used tires, rock piles, old culvert sections, drain tile, or woven fence wire can also be utilized as a suitable base for a brush pile. Once the base of the brush pile is established, other logs, trimmed branches, or even discarded Christmas trees can be stacked against the base, stump side toward the center. Breaking and bending lower branches of a tree to the ground is another quick and relately easy was to construct a brush pile.

Some sort of base for the brush pile creates openings in the interior allowing wildlife species to move inside the brush pile. Over time, the pile will begin to sag and require additional branches to maintain effectiveness.

"Living" brush piles can be constructed using one or a number of trees, either deciduous or coniferous. Living brush piles are created by cutting a live tree (or trees) one-half to two-thirds through the trunk, then pushing the tree over on its side. Leaving a portion of the trunk and bark intact allows the tree to continue growing while enhancing the cover value of the pile. Cut the tree trunk two to three feet above the ground to provide a suitable base for the brush pile. Several trees in a concentrated area can be cut in this manner and felled in sequence to form a criss-cross living brush pile. Since living brush piles are normally not as dense a traditional brush piles, stack additional branches against the felled tree(s) to increase the cover density.

Once established, enhance your habitat by planting wildlife foods around the edges. Raspberry, climbing roses, and climbing vines will grow over the brush pile, further increasing its sheltering ability. And, moisture collected from trapped snow and precipitation will improve the growing conditions for these plants.

By Evin Oneale, edited from Wyoming Game and Fish Department's Habitat Extension Bulletin #11

Rabbits and Hares

There are three main species in the geographic area covered by this book: The cottontail, snowshoe hare, and the jackrabbit. The mountain cottontail is a small rabbit often found around homes, farms, and ranch dwellings. They are the most likely culprit of the three when a vegetable or flower garden is being attacked.

They are active in the early and late hours of the day, feeding quietly around and under brush. They nest in a small burrow or hollow, producing as many as five litters in a summer.

Snowshoe hares look similar to cottontails but their hind feet are very large, and in winter the animals turn white with black ear-tips. In spring and summer they eat grass and forbs and in winter live on twigs and bark. They are usually inactive during the day but may be frightened out of shrubs or landscaping.

The white-tailed jackrabbit is a large hare with big hind feet and very large ears. It also turns white in winter and is largely nocturnal. They prefer open country and seldom gather around residential areas in any numbers. They are commonly killed on highways as they feed at night on succulent roadside vegetation.

All three of these species are important raptor and predator food. They seldom occur in sufficient numbers to cause any real damage to property or vegetation, and can be controlled with a fence of one-inch or smaller mesh that is flush with the ground or buried several inches. The top should reach a foot or more above anticipated snow levels. Individual trees and shrubs can be protected with sheet metal wrapped loosely around the trunk.